the wine experience

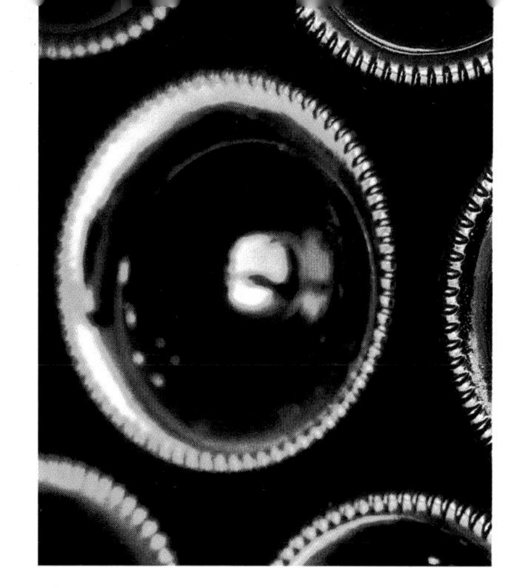

the wine experience

a new method which will revolutionise
the practice and art of wine-tasting

gérard basset

To Trich & Malcom
Santé
G Basset

KYLE CATHIE LIMITED

I would like to dedicate this book to my wife Nina, without whose tremendous support and continual encouragement I would have not been able to reach even the halfway mark. My young son Romané for his smiley faces that cheered me up when I felt a bit tense. My partner and friend Robin Hutson for the constant support he gave me during this enterprise. He ensured that I had no unnecessary worries at work, directed my way and outside work has been a fabulous friend. Frances Barnes who strongly incited me to do the book and kept encouraging me. Last but by no means least, my dog Merlot for giving me the opportunity to let loose my inspiration during our daily walk in the forest.

First published in Great Britain in 2000 by
Kyle Cathie Limited
122 Arlington Road
NW1 7HP

ISBN 1 85626 365 7

Senior Editor: Helen Woodhall
Editorial Assistant: Georgina Burns
Designer: Geoff Hayes
Production: Lorraine Baird and Sha Huxtable

A Cataloguing In Publication record for this title is available from the British Library.

Colour separations by Colourscan, Singapore
Printed and bound in Singapore by Tien Wah Press

contents

introduction

Even though I was born in France I had very little opportunity to become interested in wine before I moved to England in my mid-twenties. My family mostly drank ordinary wines, often cut with water, and none of my teenage friends' parents had any connections with wine. In those days the nearest I came to any sort of wine education was watching a stage of the Tour de France going through some famous vineyards on TV.

I owe my love of wine to Victor, a restaurant manager, who, having just joined the restaurant where I was working as a waiter, put me in charge of wine service because I was the only Frenchman on the staff. Determined to prove I was worth the faith he placed in me I took my new role ever so seriously and plunged into an endless journey of wine discovery. The restaurant was in Lyndhurst in the New Forest and had a decent wine list consisting of wines from several countries. A Frenchman learning about wine in England might seem surprising at first, but given the immense range of wines available in the UK, it certainly isn't a bad place to start.

People who begin learning a subject on their own do not always choose the appropriate method and so it was for me. Initially I did a lot of reading about wine but little actual wine-tasting. Soon I could draw, with great precision, maps of wine areas and recite the names of their grapes but was completely unable to describe the flavours of their wines. I really became aware of how patchy my budding wine knowledge was during the first sommelier competition I entered. I did surprisingly well for a beginner but I was let down by a mediocre performance in the tasting section. It was purely by luck that I started taking part in this type of event, but I immediately fell for the thrill of competing. So, as wine tasting is an important part of such competitions, I knew I had to improve dramatically to stand any chance of winning.

From being a topic I felt I had to master, wine-tasting became an absorbing passion. I looked for books and courses on the subject and spent time tasting wines with experienced tasters; anything that could help me to develop my tasting skill. Not surprisingly, the more I progressed the more enjoyable it became.

Grape-growing and wine-making techniques are improving all the time, and as a result produce new flavours and experiences, so that our understanding of wine and its language is continually evolving. Impressions and reactions produced by wine-tasting are so numerous and varied that tasting never fails to surprise me.

When I passed the Master of Wine examination I was awarded the Bollinger Medal for the best tasting performance among that year's successful candidates. It was, of course, an immense satisfaction, especially considering my modest start in that field. But even then I knew that there is always room for improvement.

After so many years of close involvement with, and enthusiasm for, wine-tasting I wanted to share my passion with others, hence this book, in which I will address every aspect of wine-tasting from the straightforward issues to more controversial ones. I have written it in plain English, avoiding jargon as far as possible, so that it will be readily understood by and appeal to both the keen beginner and the more experienced taster. I do not expect everyone to agree with my opinions, but, more importantly, I will be well satisfied if this book encourages others to explore the delights of wine-tasting.

1962

what is wine-tasting?

chapter 1

the concept

Just as listening is different from hearing, so is tasting from drinking. Drinking is a natural action, which, most of the time, is accomplished without much thought. Wine-tasting, however, demands that we pay attention to what we are doing. It is essential for wine professionals to master this discipline, but it can also greatly benefit anyone who simply enjoys the occasional glass of wine.

Assessing the character and quality of wine is a necessary task that wine professionals are routinely required to perform. Producers regularly taste their wines during wine-making to check on their progress, ready to intervene if need be: for instance, if a wine-maker decides that the wine has reached the desired level of oak flavour, he might decide that it is time to draw it out of the oak barrels. Wine merchants frequently take part in wine-tasting sessions either to select their wines or to present them to customers. Sommeliers, for their part, would have great difficulty recommending and describing wines to diners if they had never even sampled them. As for journalists, one can hardly imagine them waxing lyrical about a particular wine if they had not tried it before putting pen to paper.

Wine-tasting is such a fundamental activity of the wine trade that an official glass (the ISO tasting glass) was created in France in the early 1970s. The intention was not only to provide tasters with the ideal tool but also to increase the consistency of tasting exercises by having everyone use identical glasses during a session.

Of course, quite apart from wine-tasting, wine can be analysed very precisely: all sorts of sophisticated instruments are available for measuring the levels of the principal components of wine. (For more about wine composition see pages 180–3.) Laboratory analyses are particularly important in allowing wine-makers to detect potential problems. For instance a wine showing a slightly higher than normal level of volatile acidity might alert the wine-maker to the possibility of bacterial contamination. In addition, the amounts of some elements, such as sulphur dioxide (an almost indispensable wine preservative), need to be known accurately for legal reasons, as there are maximum permitted levels according to the style of wine.

Knowing the composition of a wine can give wine professionals a fairly clear idea as to its type and style but it is no replacement for wine-tasting. The analysis of a sound wine will not tell them if this wine is

CHÂTEAU
CRU CLASSÉ
CONTROLÉE
DÉPOSÉ

ordinary, good or even exceptional. In fact two wines could show almost identical results from their laboratory analysis, but one could nevertheless taste much better than the other. A simple analogy is to think of a car. Reading technical information on a car will indicate its category, and a thorough service will show us if the engine is in good order or not, but only driving it will really tell us how comfortable, pleasant or racy the car is.

For casual wine drinkers, information on the myriad wines available is easily obtainable nowadays. Thanks to books, magazines, newspapers, TV, the Internet and almost any other media you can think of, good, sound advice is not scarce. None the less, a basic understanding of wine-tasting is something that many of us lack but which most of us would find useful. How many people feel ill at ease in a restaurant when asked to taste the wine they have just ordered? Would they always know if the wine is sound or if it has a fault? Even in a less formal environment, a little competence in wine-tasting can prove useful. At home, even though we do not expect to be judged by our guests, serving a really mediocre wine (and by mediocre I am not necessarily referring to its price!), might rather spoil an otherwise very successful meal.

However, while knowing how to taste wine can be very helpful, its true purpose is to augment the enjoyment this wonderful drink can give. Following some simple advice is often enough not to miss out on great vinous moments. In effect, mastering wine-tasting is akin to having learned to swim in that a whole new realm of exciting sensations is suddenly opened up to us. Genuine appreciation of wine has nothing to do with being a wine bore or a wine snob!

The principles of wine-tasting can be assimilated quickly. It is amazing how fast you can learn once you turn your mind to it. Of course I am not saying that in no time at all you will be describing any wine in the unique style of TV pundit Oz Clarke or that you will be capable of matching the expertise of the renowned wine critic Robert Parker; nevertheless you will soon be surprised at your progress. Just as a few dancing lessons wouldn't transform any of us into Fred Astaire or Ginger Rogers, they would certainly be enough to supply the confidence some of us lack!

Now that the concept of wine-tasting is clearer, let's move on to its practical aspect, from the point of view of both the taster and the organiser. After all, you might start going to tastings and then move on to organise your own, even if only in a small way.

In its most basic form you could organise a wine-tasting almost anywhere; you need just a bottle of wine, a bottle-opener and a glass. However, just as you will dance better on a proper dance floor wearing the right type of clothes, so you will taste wine more effectively if some very simple requirements are met. The venue for the tasting needs to be well lit; daylight or artificial lighting are fine as long as they provide a clear light, but beware of some fluorescent lighting which can distort the colour of the wines.

Jacques Puisais, a French oenologist, has carried out some experiments which show that the colour of the room could influence our perception. Suffice to say that light colours are preferable, as dark ones make colour appreciation difficult, while a very bright environment might be distracting and affect the concentration of the tasters.

The room needs to be well aired to avoid any stale smells and it must be free from any external odours so that the tasters can concentrate on the smell of the wine alone. For instance wine-tasting close to a cheeseboard or in a room that has just been repainted would be less than ideal. The ambient temperature should be around 18–22°C (64–72°F). Tasting in the cold is not much fun but, equally, tasting in very warm conditions is unpleasant; consequently if there are many tasters present have the room temperature at the lower end of the scale as their body heat will slightly increase the overall temperature. Although space is not a crucial issue, each taster still needs to feel comfortable, so do not cram too many people into a small room. Finally, just as doing crosswords is easier in a quiet location, noise should be kept to a minimum.

If you are doing the tasting at home with a few friends you most probably will not need to make much adjustment: after all, good lighting or the perfect temperature should not be too difficult to obtain in your own surroundings. If you are organising the tasting in an unfamiliar place, such as a hotel function room, it is worth anticipating any potential problems as, particularly with a large-scale tasting, they will take longer to rectify. So to ensure a professional, efficient tasting for your guests or customers inspect the room thoroughly beforehand and give any necessary instructions.

Very elaborate tasting rooms can be found in modern wine-making schools. In the best examples they provide each taster with an individual booth, excellent lighting conditions, a sink with running water and the best equipment. These tasting rooms are very functional places but tend to be used mostly by wine chemists as they can feel very clinical.

location

The most indispensable piece of equipment is the wineglass. As I mentioned earlier, an official tasting glass does exist, which is available from specialist wine outlets or even from some high street wine merchants. New designs of glasses specifically made for wine-tasting come on to the market regularly. The glass company *Les Impitoyables* produce what they call *Le Taster*, while the famous Austrian glass producer George Riedel has his own version of a tasting glass. However, although it is not essential to have these particular glasses in order to taste wine correctly, you do need to consider a few important points when choosing wineglasses.

A good wineglass should have a stem. This will allow you to keep your hand away from the bowl of the glass, thus avoiding any fingerprints on it which might impair the appearance of the wine and any alteration in the temperature of the wine from the warmth of the hand. In addition, a glass with a stem is much easier to swirl (swirling is an important aspect of wine-tasting: see the technique section in chapter 3 pages 62–79).

The bowl should be tulip-or egg-shaped, or at least elongated and narrow at the top. This form allows more aromas to be retained in the glass and minimises interference from external smells. Also, you are much less likely to spill wine when swirling this type of glass than one with a wide rim.

The wineglass should be made of clear, thin glass. It might seem obvious to say that only a very clear glass should be use to judge the appearance of wine, but many wineglasses are produced with thick-cut designs or even using tinted glass so that a good visual examination is difficult. It is also true that a wine tastes better from a thin glass; apparently this is because the flow of wine is better directed on to the tongue and into the palate.

Its size should be generous enough that when filled to a third of its volume it holds sufficient wine to assess and allows swirling to be done without any risk of spillage. A good capacity for a tasting glass ranges between 250ml (9 fl oz) and 350ml (12 fl oz), which is larger than the official tasting glass (the ISO tasting glass has a capacity of around 215ml/7½ fl oz), but is not too small to be used for drinking wine with a meal.

Washing glasses should be done without delay; if you leave dirty glasses overnight you will need to use more detergent than if you wash them straight away. I do not say this for reasons of economy but because minute

equipment

traces of detergent can easily remain in the glass, and adversely affect both the appearance and taste of the wine. Use lots of hot, clean water with just a touch of washing-up liquid, followed by a thorough rinse. Some professionals are against wiping glasses with a cloth for fear of contamination. Personally I do prefer to polish them because I think it is the best way to get really shining glasses free from any marks. I use two clean, dry cloths (the kind that produce hardly any fluff), the first to get rid of the moisture and the second for the real polishing. Although it is true that even what looks like a clean cloth can carry bacteria I believe that the risk is minimal. Because of its relatively high acidity and alcohol content wine is a very unfavourable medium for the survivial of harmful micro-organisms; once the wine is poured into the glass a sort of natural sterilisation takes place. In any case, pathogens are not just found on cloths but can simply exist in the atmosphere.

Glasses should not be stored in cardboard boxes as they will take on the distinctive smell of cardboard or even a slightly musty odour. Keeping them in a cupboard is fine, but if they have not been used for a while it is safer to wash them again before use. A worthwhile habit is always to smell the glass before pouring the wine: this might prevent you, on occasion, from blaming a fault on the wine when in fact it is the glass that has a problem.

The number of glasses required will be determined by the type of tasting and, obviously, the number of tasters. The tasting can be run as a discussion, either tutored or not. This type of tasting generally focuses on a small number of wines, say from six to twelve. The idea is to make comparisons between the wines, so it is essential to allow one glass of each wine for every taster. So if you have eight wines and fifteen people, including a lecturer, you will need 120 glasses. For more open types of tasting, such as at a wine fair, the number of wines is generally much greater. A few hundred wines could be on show, and even though tasters do not have to taste them all, they still sample a high number. Nevertheless one glass per taster is considered perfectly adequate (but plan for some additional ones to be on the safe side). Tasters tend to keep the same glass for the duration of the tasting, and simply rinse their glass as they go along tasting wines and writing notes.

Before going any further I would just like to mention an item that is not a glass but whose sole purpose is to be used for tasting wine: the tastevin. Normally made in silver, it looks like a shallow cup, but nowadays it is only used by a few traditional wine producers since it is not as well suited for wine-tasting as a tasting glass. It can be helpful, though, in a dark cellar for appraising the depth of colour in a wine when it is held next to a candle. Also, being in silver, it is much stronger than a glass and can easily fit into a pocket. This beautiful object is often seen on the emblems of many wine associations because of the traditions it represents. Call me a romantic if you like, but I find it sad when I see one used as an ashtray!

The next item you need is a good bottle-opener. There is a surprisingly large range of these available; in fact, amazing collections have been gathered by real aficionados. A book could be written on the corkscrew alone (it may already have been) but I will simply mention some of the most interesting examples.

The Screwpull Pocket Model, like the standard Screwpull Model, is easy to use, as the Teflon-coated spiral, thanks to its endless screw system, ensures that very little effort is required to pull the cork. The long spiral can cope with even the lengthiest of corks (although it can pierce them too). In addition it takes up less room in a pocket than the standard Screwpull Model and it is fun to reassemble. Screwpull also produces a Lever Model, which is very practical for opening a large number of bottles quickly (for example at large functions) because the lever system cuts the time spent on turning the spiral; nevertheless I would not use it on old bottles as it can disturb the sediment with its brusque action.

The Waiter's Friend is often criticised for being difficult to use but if you have a good model you will quickly come to grips with it and find it easy to handle. It is, after all, a very clever device as it pulls the cork without too much effort once you are used to it. In a good example of a Waiter's Friend, the spiral should not be too thick to hold the cork well, and it should be long enough to provide a good leverage action. So many versions of it exist: some have spirals that are too short or too thick, or the distance between the spiral and the arm resting on the top of the bottle is all wrong, providing a poor angle for pulling the cork, so beware of the cheap ones.

The Rolls Royce of the Waiter's Friend is commonly acknowledged to be the Château-Laguiole, while a new Waiter's Friend exists where the arm for resting on top

of the bottle is equipped with two positions, one for pulling halfway and one for the final pulling.

A less well-known corkscrew is the Puig-Pull, named after its inventor Mr Puig. It pulls the cork gently, thanks to a spiral activated by a system with teeth, and can be used with only one hand.

The last opener I want to single out is the Two-Bladed one. As the two fixed parallel blades are inserted between the inside of the neck of the bottle and the cork it has the peculiarity of not piercing the cork and therefore prevents bits of cork floating into the wine. It works by turning and pulling the opener gently while keeping the bottle still. It takes a few attempts to feel confident with it.

Although not crucial, it is worth mentioning that the capsule should be cut neatly under the lip of the neck of the bottle. This prevents the wine from coming into contact with the capsule during pouring. Moulds can grow between the capsule and the bottle during ageing, so by taking off a big part of the capsule and wiping the top of the bottle thoroughly there is no risk of mould contaminating the wine.

Not the most exciting of objects, spittoons are nevertheless compulsory if the tasters are not to be legless by the end of the tasting. Ice-buckets are well suited for use as spittoons but many other containers will do just as well. Make sure they are fairly large and deep and line the base with sawdust or some shredded paper to reduce splashing. They should be positioned in safe places and emptied regularly. For a small group of tasters one spittoon per person is ideal; in bigger tastings spittoons are normally shared by several tasters.

Tasting sheets or, at the very least, blank sheets of paper, should always be provided for writing tasting notes. White paper tasting sheets are great as they also provide an excellent background to assess the wine's appearance. For formal tastings, where tasters are seated and usually have more time for each wine, it is customary to have fairly elaborate tasting sheets. The full identity of the wine is given with perhaps some

additional information such as its price and the name of the company that sells it. Plenty of space should be allocated next to each wine for tasters to write their comments. Columns with the headings Appearance, Nose, Taste and Overall Impression can be helpful, but just a large blank space next to each wine will do equally well. In a more casual tasting, tasting sheets are still required but perhaps with slightly less blank space, especially if a lot of wines are on display; normally the more wines tasted the more abbreviated the notes. For tastings where everyone is standing you might consider supplying clipboards to make note-taking easier. Most people who go to tastings will have their own pens or pencils, but it is worth having spare ones just in case.

Still water (mineral or tap) should be available at any tasting. Glasses might need rinsing and many tasters like to clean their palates every so often. It is recommended that you drink some water when you are changing from one style of wine to another (such as going from a set of light red wines to a set of fuller red wines), but not between two wines that you are comparing (too much water can interfere with and alter your perception). Bread and dry biscuits are also appreciated by tasters to give them a welcome break from wine.

Naturally, tables and chairs are needed for a seated tasting. Large white paper mats are handy not only to protect the table but also to give a good background when judging the appearance of the wines. For a standing tasting, tables are required on which to display the wines. My only advice here – no more than common sense – is to make sure that the tables are very stable and are not overloaded with bottles to reduce any chance of an accident.

the wines

There are no hard and fast rules as to what types of wine should be presented at a tasting, but in general it is more satisfactory if the tasting has a purpose. Comparison between two similar styles of wines is a classic topic: for instance Barbaresco versus Barolo. Presenting wines from the new vintage of a particular area is another popular type of tasting, as in the New Zealand 1999 Marlborough Sauvignon Blanc. Tastings organised by wine merchants for their customers simply present their own portfolio without any specific links between wines. The possibilities are endless but the more appealing tastings tend to have a theme.

The number of wines included is determined by the objectives and set-up of the tasting. Focused seated tastings are better if the number of wines does not go above fifteen. Beyond that number it becomes difficult to carry on writing long and precise tasting notes. At larger tastings with a looser theme, where tasters walk freely from stand to stand, the number of wines is normally much higher and is simply dictated by what the organiser wishes to show.

Twelve to fifteen measures of wine per bottle is a good figure to work on to calculate the number of bottles required. For a seated tasting the estimate is relatively easy once you know both the number of wines and tasters. When a very large number of wines is on show, not all will be tasted by every single participant; so if you are going to be behind a stand

think how many samples you can reasonably serve per hour and anticipate which wines are going to be the most popular. But whatever the type of tasting, always allow for corked bottles. It never fails to amaze me when I go to a tasting and I hear the lecturer announcing: 'Sorry for the very small amount of wine in glass number seven but one bottle was corked.' Other than when dealing with rare wines where the number of bottles available is limited, the tasting organiser should have additional bottles of each wine on the side, particularly if the tasters are going to be numerous. Only open the minimum number of bottles needed to avoid wastage.

Wines should be served in the best possible conditions. Unless you are in your own home temperatures are not always easy to control. Fridges might not work properly or may be too small to accommodate all the wines, or the room might be very warm with no air-conditioning. So if you are booking a tasting room, inspect it in advance to ensure the presence of an efficient fridge, air-conditioning and the availability of ice. At a standing tasting, where the same bottle may be consumed very slowly and remain open for a considerable time, it is important that the wine is maintained at the correct temperature, as far as possible, throughout the tasting. Temperatures to aim for range from 10°C–14°C (50–57°F) for white wine and from 14°C–18°C (57–64°F) for red wine. Fridges, ice-buckets and wine coolers are all excellent for maintaining the desired temperature of white wine, but if a bottle stays in the same place for too long you might have to swap it from fridge to table or vice versa.

Finally, every single bottle of wine should be tasted in order to withdraw any faulty bottles (see wine faults in chapter 4 pages 96–99) before they can be served. Among the potential defects in a bottle of wine, cork taint is by far the most common. We can only hope that the problem will be eradicated in the next ten or twenty years. Sadly, it is not unusual at tastings to be served corked wine or to find some on a stand. It is always possible to miss a bottle with a very faint defect (if it has been tasted too cold or too quickly) but I find it hard to see how a badly corked wine can escape the attention of the person in charge.

Even if it is your job you should only go to a tasting if you feel well both physically and mentally. If you have a cold or a bad headache you will not do justice to the wines. Equally, while serious anxieties might not stop you from being able to taste, I doubt you will be able to concentrate properly. Avoid consuming spicy food or strong drinks such as gin or black coffee just before a tasting session, as these will taint your palate for a little while. The best time to taste is just before a meal when you feel slightly hungry.

Wine-tasting might not have a very rigid code of conduct, but there are still some important rules. Smoking during a tasting or wearing strong perfume are complete no-nos. Commenting loudly on the wines while others are still tasting can be really infuriating. Quite simply you should avoid doing anything to unsettle other tasters; after all, you would not like to be on the receiving end of such behaviour. And if you do not want to torture yourself later by wondering what strange comments you might have made, remember that spittoons are there to be used. As for dress code, unless specified you can wear whatever you wish, but do not put on your best dress or smartest suit, and avoid light colours, for accidents can always happen.

the tasters

chapter 2

what is wine?

definition

The official EU definition of wine, several pages long, is cleverly summarised in Jancis Robinson's *Oxford Companion to Wine*: 'The alcoholic beverage obtained from the fermentation of the juice of freshly gathered grapes, the fermentation taking place in the district of origin according to local tradition and practice.'

Wine is a fairly natural product. Most of its components derive from the grape and from the effects of fermentation. Wine-makers can interfere in some measure by increasing or decreasing slightly some of the natural elements of the grape; adding extra sugar to grape juice, supplementing or reducing the natural level of acidity of grape juice or wine, or removing a fraction of the water content of grape juice or wine are the most common interventions. Substances such as clay, egg white or gelatine are normally used to clarify and stabilise the wine, but they do not remain in the finished wine (other than perhaps as a tiny residue). Sulphur dioxide, a protective and preservative agent, is almost always added to grape juice and wine. All these operations are strictly regulated by national laws.

Thanks to modern technology we have a pretty clear idea of a wine's make-up. For those interested in the subject, some of the most important components are listed on pages 180–3 where their role in regard to taste is explained. The exact proportions of those components, in any wine, determines its type and style and in addition affects its quality.

A combination of three factors is used to designate the type of wine. The first is the colour of the wine, being either red, rosé or white. The second depends on the method of production. A wine can be still (sometimes referred to as table wine in countries outside the EU), sparkling or fortified. Still wine means that the wine has not been strengthened with additional alcohol and also that it contains no excess carbon dioxide (CO_2). Sparkling wine means that some CO_2 has either been added or not allowed to escape and is kept in the wine under pressure. Fortified wine means that alcohol has been added to increase its natural level. The third factor is the level of sweetness, ranging from bone dry to extremely sweet. So we can have a still dry white wine such as a Pinot Grigio from Veneto, a sparkling dry rosé like many from Champagne, or a sweet red fortified wine such as a vintage port. These are just three possible combinations. Although when a wine is referred to by its type, very often it is shortened to just one or two of these factors, as in a red wine or a dry white wine. The understanding being, in the case of red wines, that the great majority of them are dry and still, therefore only if referring to a red wine that is neither still nor dry would the entire description be used. Similarly, dry white implies that the wine is still.

Sometimes a wine type is also referred to according to its alcoholic level, which is in fact dependent on the method of production. Even though it is an important aspect of wine, it is not much used because the vast majority of still wines are of similar alcohol level (around 12–14 per cent) and probably also because it is not seen as vital information for most wine drinkers. Nevertheless for people who have good reason to be concerned about their alcohol intake, low-alcohol or non-alcoholic wine is readily available. Low-alcohol strength in wine is very strictly regulated by laws defining categories such as 'alcohol-free' (no more than 0.05 per cent), 'de-alcoholised' (no more than 0.5 per cent), and 'low alcohol' (no more than 1.2 per cent).

More people are now interested in another category of wines, the so-called organic wines (officially: wines made from organically grown grapes). These are made from grapes produced without the use of chemical fertilisers, herbicides or pesticides (although sulphur and copper sprays are permitted to fight fungal diseases). Certain rules for wine-making, such as lower levels of sulphur dioxide, also apply. While commendable, making wines in this way does not automatically make them taste different or better. (In fact many conventional wine producers apply part or all of their methods.) Therefore on taste alone organic wine cannot be regarded a separate type of wine.

Defining the style of a wine is less clear-cut; in fact, it is no more than a subdivision of the wine type. It is usually based on the smell of the wine, or its 'mouthfeel', which is a combination of its texture and body, or a combination of its smell and a particular detail of the wine-making. Examples of wine style based on smell include: aromatic dry white (lots of aromas), or spicy red (with plenty of spicy odours). Mouthfeel examples include: crisp white (feeling fresh and lively in the mouth), smooth red (perceived as having a soft texture), light-bodied (feeling light on the palate) or full-bodied (feeling full on the palate). Examples of smell resulting from wine-making techniques include: oaky dry white (smelling of the new oak barrels in which it was matured) or botrytised wine (having complex odours of honey and roasted fruit from the botrytis-affected grapes – a type of beneficial rot which concentrates the sweetness and produces some particular flavours – from which the wine was made). These are the most commonly used definitions of wine style, but as there are no real rules all sorts of expressions are used, from 'New World style' and 'traditional style', to vaguer ones such as 'sexy wine'.

style

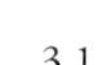

Since it is such a fundamental issue of wine-tasting, a whole chapter is dedicated to the quality of wine. Let's just say at the moment that the overall smell and texture of wine are two extremely important aspects of its quality. Vocabulary to describe quality is no different from that used in other fields: words such as exceptional, outstanding, excellent, superior, average, ordinary, mediocre or awful are just a few examples drawn from a long list of possibilities. However whereas there might be little disagreement as to a wine's type (a very dry white is just that) or even its style (a smooth red will certainly have been found smooth by the majority of tasters), this is not always the case with quality. Indeed someone might rate highly a wine that you find just plain ordinary (see the competition section of chapter 5 pages 103–19).

quality

major influences on type, style and quality

As you can imagine, thousands of elements, starting with soil preparation even before the vines are planted right up to the bottling line and long thereafter, all combine to play a part in shaping the taste of each wine. Since this book is not about wine production, I simply intend to highlight those aspects that have the most obvious effects. For readers wanting to know more about wine production a very good book to start with is *The Art and Science of Wine* by James Halliday and Hugh Johnson.

grape variety

The three most important elements in a grape variety in relation to the overall taste of the wine are the colour of its skin, its flavour profile and the composition of its juice.

A grape is referred to as either white or red depending on the colour of its skin, although in reality the skin's colour is closer to green-yellow for white grapes and black-blue-pink for red ones. White wines can be produced from the classic varieties of either white or red grapes, since the colour of their juice is similar, and the skins are not used. None the less, in most cases white wines are made from white grapes, a notable exception being white champagne for which a large proportion of red grapes are used. Red wines get their colour from the extraction of the colouring pigments in the grape skins during fermentation; red wines therefore cannot be made without red grapes.

Each variety of grapes has a specific flavour profile. Some will give wines a smell with a distinct floral character, while others will impart aromas similar to those of familiar fruits. In addition, some grapes have more flavour than others, ranging from very aromatic down to fairly neutral. Of white grape varieties, Gewürztraminer and Muscat are typical examples of very aromatic grapes, Pinot Gris and Sauvignon Blanc are aromatic ones, Chardonnay or Sémillon are more semi-aromatic and Aligote and Ugni Blanc tend to be considered as neutral ones. Of course this is just a guideline; for instance Riesling, a very aromatic grape, can produce both highly aromatic and more neutral wines. Red grapes are seldom referred to as very aromatic; instead we talk more of aromatic (Pinot Noir) or vinous (Carignan) for those with less flavour.

The composition of the grape juice is crucial in forming the body and texture of the wine. It largely consists of water with sugars, acids, some colouring pigments and tannins (whose levels are higher if stems and skins are left during fermentation), and several other natural elements in minute quantities, such as minerals. Each variety of grape shows differences in the composition of its juice, with some, for example, naturally having more acidity than others.

The grape variety has a considerable impact on the

final wine; indeed the composition of the juice will provide the type and the style of the wine, and both the composition and the quality of the juice will determine the overall quality of the wine. As we have seen, red wine requires red grapes. Crisp white wines cannot easily be made with every variety of white grapes; Marsanne or Gewürztraminer for instance, are less than ideally suited for this style. A talented winemaker might be able to produce a good wine from a neutral grape variety, but he or she will never achieve a superb wine; even the best examples of Ugni Blanc or Carignan wines are rarely considered fine wines. Because the grape plays such an important role in the taste of any wine, a tasting profile of some of the major grapes is given in the last section of this chapter on pages 42–53.

location

CLIMATE

The climate is a crucial element that gives the vineyard many of its specific properties. It is determined principally by latitude but land mass, altitude, proximity to water, and surface features of the land also play a significant role in shaping it.

Vines require a certain amount of heat, light and water to produce ripe grapes. In general the best results are achieved under a temperate climate with a fairly cold winter, a spring that is not too frosty, and some warm but fairly dry conditions for both summer and early autumn.

Climatic conditions are very significant in determining the type and style of the wine. The cooler the conditions the less sugar and more acidity the grapes will have, giving lighter and crisper wines; the warmer the conditions the more sugar and less acidity the grapes will have, giving fuller and rounder wines. As they require more heat than white grapes, red grapes do not flourish in a very cool climate; for instance Syrah would struggle to produce ripe grapes in England. However the English climate is well suited to the production of light, aromatic white wines.

Quality is also determined by the prevailing climate. Extreme conditions tend to produce unbalanced wines: too cool and the wines might have a coarse texture with some unripe flavours; too warm and the wines might have a flabby structure and lack of flavours. For example grapes grown in the hot Central Valley of California very rarely produce wines of the same finesse as from those grown in the more hospitable climate of the Napa Valley, also in California.

SOIL

Many types of soil are suitable for the development of the vines' roots. The better ones are well drained but still capable of retaining moisture and are not too

fertile, to avoid vegetative rather than fruit growth.

Very few subjects are as controversial in the world of wine as the issue of soil, which the French refer to as *terroir*. Technically speaking, the *terroir* does not include just the soil, but also takes into account the topography and local climatic conditions. However, in the usual concept of the *terroir* the soil plays the leading role. Indeed, in many French areas, where often the topography and the micro-climate of two neighbouring pieces of land appear very similar, one may be regarded as being much better than the other because of the supposedly special chemical composition of its soil. And if quality is not the issue, the difference of character between the wines will often be attributed to the soil chemistry of the vineyard. To prove it you just need to speak to a French wine producer. They are bound to tell you, at one time or another, that the unique flavours in their wines are definitively due to their very special limestone or granite *terroir*. They may be right, but it could also be that it has more to do with a combination of the special micro-climate in the vineyard, the moderate fertility and the drainage quality of the soil rather than the direct effect of some specific minerals in the soil. In truth it is not clear to what extent soil chemistry affects the character of a wine. Scientists are continually working to try to improve our understanding of this subject. So it can be rather annoying to hear some wine experts, often French ones, preaching religiously on the exact consequences that the minerals in the soil have for a wine's flavours. In addition, when listening to them, it seems that only France has been blessed with the right mix of minerals for grape growing. Don't get me wrong, I love French wines and have great respect for the many talented French producers but France is not alone in having great soils and, by extension, great *terroirs.*

None the less there is no doubt that soil in general, whether its physical or chemical attributes, plays an important role in terms of the quality of the finished wine. In some instances it can accelerate or delay ripening, leading to beneficial or disastrous consequences for the quality of the wine. It also has an influence on the type and style of the wine. For instance some soils seem better suited to the production of sparkling wines, as in Champagne, and the soil of the Graves area in Bordeaux usually gives slightly lighter red wines than that of the Médoc.

vintage

Weather patterns are not static and conditions can differ slightly, or occasionally considerably, from one year to the next in the same location, so that the character of the grapes and consequently of the wines can vary. This explains the concept and importance of the vintage, where a given year's production is deemed to be an excellent or a poor vintage.

The weather affects the quality of the wine; for instance heavy rainfall just before and during the harvest are never synonymous with great quality as rain dilutes the grape juice and encourages the spread of fungal diseases. However both the style and the type of wine will also be affected by the vintage conditions. Warm weather during the last few weeks before harvest is likely to give smoother red wines than in a colder year, and if this warm weather carries on well into the autumn sweeter wines will be produced.

production

IN THE VINEYARD

Work in the vineyard and in the winery both influence the type, style and quality of the wine. Working towards harvesting healthy and fully ripened grapes entails looking after the soil, nurturing the vines and tending the grapes. To allow for good root development both the structure and the composition of

the soil need to be maintained. Vines have to be trained and pruned to optimise their cultivation. The foliage and the developing grapes require constant attention, whether spraying, thinning or trimming. Finally, when the grapes are ripe, they can be picked either manually or mechanically.

Evidently, incompetent or careless management of the soil and the vines will result in grapes that are unripe, diluted or in poor sanitary condition with disastrous consequences for the future quality of the wines. Work in the vineyard has less important an influence on the type and style of wine than on the quality. In the same area, grapes destined to make a red wine and those for a white wine will require a similar maintenance, although a few variations do exist.

IN THE WINERY

It is a long process from grape gathering to the bottling line. Grape juice (referred to as the must) has first to be fermented. Then, depending on the type of wine, a rapid or slow maturation will take place, either in neutral containers such as lined cement tanks or stainless-steel vats, or, to add extra flavour, the wine will be matured partly or totally in contact with new oak, normally in small casks. Some blending might take place, and to transform this crude wine into an attractive liquid some clarification and stabilisation operations (racking, fining and filtration) will be undertaken. When it is judged that the wine is ready to drink or that nothing else will enhance it, other than possibly ageing in the bottle, the wine is packaged.

Among the major winery operations, the use of new oak is probably the most significant. In the words of Chris Foss, a wine chemist who is head of the wine programme at Plumpton College, new oak is by far the most important flavouring in wine. And if wine-makers choose to use some new oak for their wines, they then have to decide on its origin, its form, its preparation and its amount. American oak and French oak, the two most popular types, have slightly different characteristics, American normally being thought to give a fuller, more spicy flavour to the wine, while

French is thought to give it more finesse. The most common use of new oak is in the form of small barrels, called barriques, with a volume of around 225 litres (50 gallons), but bigger or smaller casks are also commonly used. In addition, casks permit more oxygen contact with the wine than stainless-steel vats, resulting in a beneficial controlled oxidation that will soften the wine. To save costs and some of the labour required by the use of barrels, it is possible to impart an oaky flavour by adding some new oak planks or oak chips to a wine tank. Of course this never gives the same result as using well-made casks. New oak casks are charred inside, and the level of charring, known as light, medium or heavy toast, will have an important impact on the flavour. Oak chips can be roasted to similar requirements. A wine can be matured with 100 per cent new oak, meaning that all the casks are brand-new, or with less than 100 per cent, when only a proportion of the casks will be new. So, depending on the selection of the oak used, the wine will have a greater or lesser oak flavour reminiscent of spice, toast and vanilla (vanillin being a natural constituent of oak). All these decisions are dictated by the preferences of the wine-maker, the market the wine is destined for, the type of wine (some aromatic grape varieties, such as Riesling, do not blend well with oak), and finally, as new oak (especially barrels) is expensive, how much the winery can afford.

Depending on the means and the aims of the winery, quality will be affected enormously by wine-making methods. It would be unrealistic to expect the quality of a low-budget, low-priced wine to challenge that of a wine on which no expense has been spared and which is to be sold at a premium price. However, the talent of the wine-maker can both diminish or accentuate the differences.

As we have just seen with the use of new oak, wine-making methods are important in determining the style and type of the wine. I would like to underline just a few wine-making practices that give a specific character to wines which are easily recognisable from taste alone.

Carbonic maceration: used for the production of light fruity red wines. Whole bunches of grapes are put into vats filled with carbon dioxide to provoke an intracellular fermentation of the berries, then after a few days the grapes are pressed and the fermentation is finished in the normal manner. This produces red wines that are less tannic, with a juicy structure and some exuberant fruity flavours often strongly reminiscent of banana.

Flavour-enhancing yeasts: often used for wines that are destined to be drunk very young. Some special strains of yeast are capable of increasing and even generating fruit flavours in some fairly non-aromatic grapes. The only problem is that those flavours disappear in the

C399
C402
C422
C423
C424
C425
C426
C428
C435
C436
C443
C444
C445
C446
C447
C448
C449
C455
C456
C457
C465
C466
C467
C468
C469
C483
C484
C492
C493
C505

wine after just a few months.

Cold fermentation: used for the production of fresh white wines. The temperatures of fermentation are controlled and maintained sufficiently low (around 15°C (58°F) or less) to give white wines their fresh flavours; but if the fermentation has been conducted at too cold a temperature and the grapes had only limited tastes to start with, it will give a flavour strongly reminiscent of sherbet and pear drops.

Malolactic fermentation: used for most red wines and some not so aromatic white wines such as many Chardonnays. The wines have a part of their acidity transformed (the malic into lactic) naturally by the action of bacteria. This softens the wines and in white wines often gives a slightly buttery flavour.

Flor maturation: used for the production of some special wines such as fino sherry or vin jaune. The wines are aged under a veil of yeasts that serves to protect them from the action of oxygen. The wines develop powerful flavours, often giving a combination of green walnut and citrus fruit with some iodine touches.

Oxidative maturation: used principally for the production of fortified wines destined for long ageing such as oloroso sherry, tawny port, many French fortified wines (Banyuls, Rivesaltes) or for Madeira (although Madeira wines are additionally matured in very warm conditions). The technique is almost the opposite of flor ageing as the wines are deliberately matured with a certain level of oxygen contact. It produces wines with a colour marked by a certain level of brownness and the flavours are often very nutty, reminiscent of toffee or even wood polish, among others.

Lee maturation: used in the production of sparkling wines but also for certain still wines. The wines are matured for a while in contact with some of the dead yeast cells from the fermentation, either in the bottle for sparkling wines or in cask for the still ones (in cask the wine is regularly stirred to increase the contact with the yeast cells). This tends to give an added smoothness to the wine and of course, in the case of high-quality sparkling wines that remain in contact with the lees for a long time, it produces a yeasty/bready type of flavour.

social environment

Apart from the more functional components of wine production, a combination of other factors – tradition, regulations, economics and enthusiasm – will also influence the type, style and quality of the wine.

Having being made, in some areas, for hundreds of years, it is scarcely surprising that wine production feels the weight of its long history. The influence of tradition is felt most strongly in long-established wine areas, a classic example being the French appellation system, which normally dictates, among other things, the type of grape varieties to be planted, as a consequence of their long usage in those areas.

Furthermore, wine complies with some very strict rules and regulations, principally for tax and health reasons, depending on each country's traditions and views on wine consumption.

In spite of wine's romantic image, the commercial reality of our modern competitive societies also affects wine production. It is evident that the price levels that producers are aiming for will have an effect on the type, style and quality of their wines.

Finally, if so much has been, and will continue to be, written about wine, it is because it requires men and women of passion and vision to produce wine that will engender all this emotion. And, while passion does not guarantee quality, great wines are rarely produced without real passion.

ageing

Partly thanks to its acidity, its alcohol and sometimes its sugar or tannin, wine is one of the few consumable goods that can keep. Ageing will not really affect the wine type, but it can have a great impact on both its style and quality. A high-quality red wine, drunk early, might often be firm in style, but a few years of bottle ageing will transform it into a rounder, smoother style.

In the best cases, an elegant, young, fruity wine will develop in several years (five, twenty or much more) of bottle ageing into a superb and complex nectar full of indescribable flavours. However not every wine turns out like that: in fact the vast majority of wines produced nowadays should be drunk within one to three years of the vintage date and will not improve once bottled.

some tasting profiles

I have not attempted to review the character of the wines from the main wine areas because it would have required too much space in a book that is not a wine atlas. However, under each grape profile I have given some famous wine areas with which the relevant grape is associated.

white grapes

CHARDONNAY

'It is Madonna, Princess Diana and Jerry Hall, all rolled into one.' This is how Tim Atkin described Chardonnay in his book on that grape. Indeed it is liked by most wine lovers. It has enough flavour to be distinctive, but not too much to be offensive. In addition, it combines extremely well with the flavours of new oak. The wines are almost always dry and often fairly full-bodied. Mango, pineapple and peach are classic flavours from wines made in a warm climate, while a cooler climate will produce flavours resembling apple and lemon. Dried fruit is also a distinctive flavour of many top Chardonnays. Butterscotch and vanilla, often associated with Chardonnay, have more to do with the use of new oak than the grape itself.

Chardonnay is planted in almost every wine-producing country. Superb examples are found in Burgundy (Chablis (usually unoaked), Meursault, Puligny-Montrachet and Chassagne-Montrachet),

Australia, California, New Zealand and Chile, but many other areas produce some excellent Chardonnays. It is an important component of many sparkling wines, including Champagne. The best ones can easily improve and keep for five to ten years.

RIESLING

Riesling is the darling of the wine writer, but unfortunately not yet of the average wine drinker. This has much to do with the fact that Riesling is often wrongly associated with the production of some off-dry wines of mediocre quality. Riesling can produce superb wines from bone dry to very sweet and because of its naturally high acidity the wines are steely and racy even in the sweet examples. The flavour spectrum is phenomenal: depending on the style and the provenance it can vary from fresh flowers to apple, lime (Australia), peach, dried apricot, rhubarb and, after a few years of bottle ageing, it will develop into lanolin, white truffle and petrol. Top Riesling wines can age and develop for more than twenty years. The best examples are produced in Germany (Mosel, Rheingau, Pfalz, Rheinhessen), Alsace, Austria (Wachau) and Australia (Clare Valley, Eden Valley).

SAUVIGNON BLANC

A very fashionable grape, producing the type of wines that you either love or hate. The wines normally have a fresh and juicy structure, and the powerful exuberant flavours have a strong herbaceous and gooseberry character. The two benchmark Sauvignon Blanc wines are those of Marlborough in New Zealand in which additional notes of passion fruit, kiwi or even tinned asparagus intermingle, and those from the Loire Valley (Sancerre, Pouilly Fumé), in which grassy, nettle (also found in some South African examples) and mineral flavours are more prominent. In California, where it is normally sold under the name of Fumé Blanc, it is often vinified with new oak, which can alter its character greatly, making it sometimes almost unrecognisable but by no means unpleasant. Because of its natural freshness it is also used as a blending partner for Sémillon in the production of sweet wines, as in the Sauternes area of Bordeaux. Produced now in several areas, the wines are in general fairly one-dimensional and, apart from a few exceptions, are best drunk in their youth.

SEMILLON

In its dominant role in the sweet wines of Bordeaux, Sémillon provides a luscious structure and beautiful flavours of roasted fruit. It is now becoming popular in a dry style in areas such as Chile, South Africa and Washington State. Australia (Hunter Valley) has been making stunning examples for quite a while. The texture is round and the flavours are often a wonderful

Sauvignon Blanc

Riesling

Chardonnay

combination of citrus, oily fruit and touches of honey and wax. Sweet or dry, great Sémillons will age well.

CHENIN BLANC

If it were not for the great examples of the Loire Valley, Chenin Blanc would not get much of a look-in. Like Riesling, it has a naturally high acidity giving the wines a certain steeliness both in the dry and sweet examples. The flavours are a mixture of quince, apple (especially bruised), marzipan and honey. Apart from the Loire, good Chenin Blancs are now produced in New Zealand. South Africa has a large surface area dedicated to Chenin Blanc (called Steen) but makes very little interesting wine from it. Top wines (sweet and dry) from the Loire such as Côteaux du Layon, Quarts de Chaume, Savennières or Vouvray can easily age for as long as the best Rieslings.

VIOGNIER

Viognier has become a trendy grape, gradually being planted more often in wine areas around the world (California, Languedoc), but its original home is in the northern Rhône (Condrieu). The wines are round, mostly dry and have powerful flavours of flowers, peach, apricot and, in some more ordinary cases, of air freshener. Some of the wines can age but they are normally at their best in their youth when they are at their most exuberant stage.

MUSCAT

Popular for its sweet wines, Muscat can also make some appealing sparkling wines (Asti) and some charming dry white wines (Alsace). Several sub-varieties of Muscat (eg. Petits Grains, Alexandria, Hamburg and Ottonel) do exist, some more elegant than others. Their common point is a unique, recognisable grapey flavour often supplemented by notes of orange blossom, elderberry, raisin, toffee and even Christmas pudding (Australian Muscat liqueur). Beautiful sweet wines are made in most wine areas with warm climatic conditions. Muscat de Beaumes-de-Venise in France, Samos in Greece, Constantia in South Africa or Muscat liqueur in Australia are just a few famous examples among the many splendid wines made from this grape. Many are very enjoyable in their youth but others will develop extremely well over several years.

other interesting white grapes

GEWURZTRAMINER

Alsace and New Zealand. Full and very rich structure in both dry and sweet wines, with a powerful nose of lychee, ginger or rose petal.

PINOT GRIS

Alsace, Germany (called Rülander) and Eastern Europe. Rich wines with peach, apricot and spice in dry and sweet wines. Lighter and far less aromatic in the Italian version, Pinot Grigio.

MARSANNE

Rhône and Australia. Round, dry wines with a slightly almond and herbal flavour, becoming quite fashionable.

ROUSSANNE

Rhône and California. Often blended with Marsanne and not too dissimilar, but with a fresher structure and more flavour, a mixture of herbs and oily fruit.

SCHEUREBE

Germany. Producing excellent dry and sweet wines with distinctive grapefruit flavours.

ALBARINO

Galicia in north-west Spain. Trendy grape producing delicate, dry wines with a floral, peachy flavour.

TORRONTES

Argentina. Attractive light-dry wines with a distinctive floral character.

ARNEIS

Piedmonte in Italy. Gives middle-weight dry wines lacking in crispness but with some appealing floral and dry fruit flavours.

red grapes

CABERNET SAUVIGNON

Arguably the greatest red grape. Jancis Robinson, in her pocket *Guide to Wine Grapes*, called it the chocolate of the wine world (she referred to Chardonnay as the vanilla). It produces wines of high quality with tremendous consistency. The many great examples have in their youth a deep colour, a powerful and solid structure with firm but ripe tannins, and they are packed with blackcurrant, blackberry, *crème de cassis* or *mûre* (specially in Chilean examples), black cherry, bell pepper, pencil lead (Médoc), mint and eucalyptus (South Australia) flavours. With ageing, and the great ones will easily go beyond the twenty years' mark, the wines become obviously rounder and develop some incredible cedary, cigar-box, tobacco and dark chocolate notes. St Estèphe, Paulliac, St-Julien and Margaux in Bordeaux; Bolgheri in Tuscany; the Napa Valley, Sonoma Valley and Santa Cruz mountains in California; Washington State; Margaret River, Coonawarra and McLaren Vale in Australia; Waiheke Island in New Zealand; Maipo in Chile and Stellenbosch in South Africa are just a few of the many areas around the world famous for quality wines produced with this grape. The complete list of the best regions for Cabernet Sauvignon is too lengthy to give here.

Cabernet Sauvignon

Shiraz

Pinot Noir

PINOT NOIR

Pinot Noir is like those mischievous teenagers whose behaviour brings parents to despair but who, on the rare occasions when they put their minds to it, prove to have the brains of young geniuses. Pinot Noir can produce a lot of ordinary but expensive wines (especially in Burgundy) but also some exceptional ones (also in Burgundy!). New World countries, California, Chile, South Africa, Australia and New Zealand, having struggled for a long time with this grape, are now regularly producing truly beautiful wines with it, and consequently almost disproving its unreliable reputation. The best Pinot Noir wines are round or supple with a silky, velvety texture. The flavours are a mixture of raspberry, wild strawberry and ripe cherry, turning, with some bottle ageing, to wonderful gamey notes. Another characteristic of Pinot Noir wines is their lighter colour when compared with wines from other classic red grape varieties. Famous areas for Pinot Noir are Gevrey-Chambertin, Chambolle-Musigny, Vosne-Romanée, Nuits-St-Georges, Pommard and Volnay in Burgundy and the cooler spots of the New World countries, for instance Carneros in California, Walker Bay in South Africa, the Yarra Valley in Australia or Martinborough and Otago in New Zealand. Like Chardonnay, it is also an important element of many sparkling wines, Champagne included. The best Pinot Noir wines will age graciously for ten years and more.

SYRAH/SHIRAZ

The come-back kid. Indeed in both its two spiritual homes of France and Australia, this superb grape has suffered some dips of popularity in the past. However it is back with a vengeance and not just in those two places. At its best Syrah, as it is called in France, or Shiraz, as it is known in Australia, can give wines with a deep colour, a powerful structure, but with a smoother texture than those from Cabernet Sauvignon, and a beautiful array of flavours including violet, raspberry, blackberry, pepper, plum, chocolate, leather and spice. The great and classic examples come from Côte-Rôtie and Hermitage in the Rhône in France, and from the Barossa Valley, McLaren Vale and the Hunter Valley in Australia. However other areas of France and Australia, as well as California, Chile and South Africa, among others, have obtained great results with it. Syrah/Shiraz wines have a great ageing potential. In Australia Shiraz is also used in the production of port-like wines and of some strange but appealing juicy red sparkling wines.

MERLOT

Apart from the wines of St-Emilion and Pomerol in Bordeaux, Merlot lived in the shadow of Cabernet Sauvignon for a long time. Then in the early 1990s scientists started to tell us how good red wine is for our health. So Merlot, with its very approachable character, became the star of the show. It gives wines of a style not too dissimilar to Cabernet Sauvignon but rounder and smoother, and consequently the two grapes are often blended to soften the solid structure of Cabernet Sauvignon. The flavours are reminiscent of plum, fruit cake and blackcurrant. It is now widely planted and a great number of excellent Merlot wines are produced in many countries, Washington State and California performing especially well. The best wines can age very well but not quite to the extent of the great Cabernet Sauvignon wines.

NEBBIOLO

The noble grape of Italy. In the Piedmonte region, especially in the Barolo and Barbaresco areas, it produces fabulous wines. The best examples have a powerful structure with firm tannins, and the flavours are a fascinating assortment of truffle, dark chocolate, prune, violet and even tar! Both in Australia and California some growers are experimenting with this grape and it should not be too long before interesting examples appear from these countries. The best Barolo and Barbaresco wines will easily keep and improve for up to twenty years.

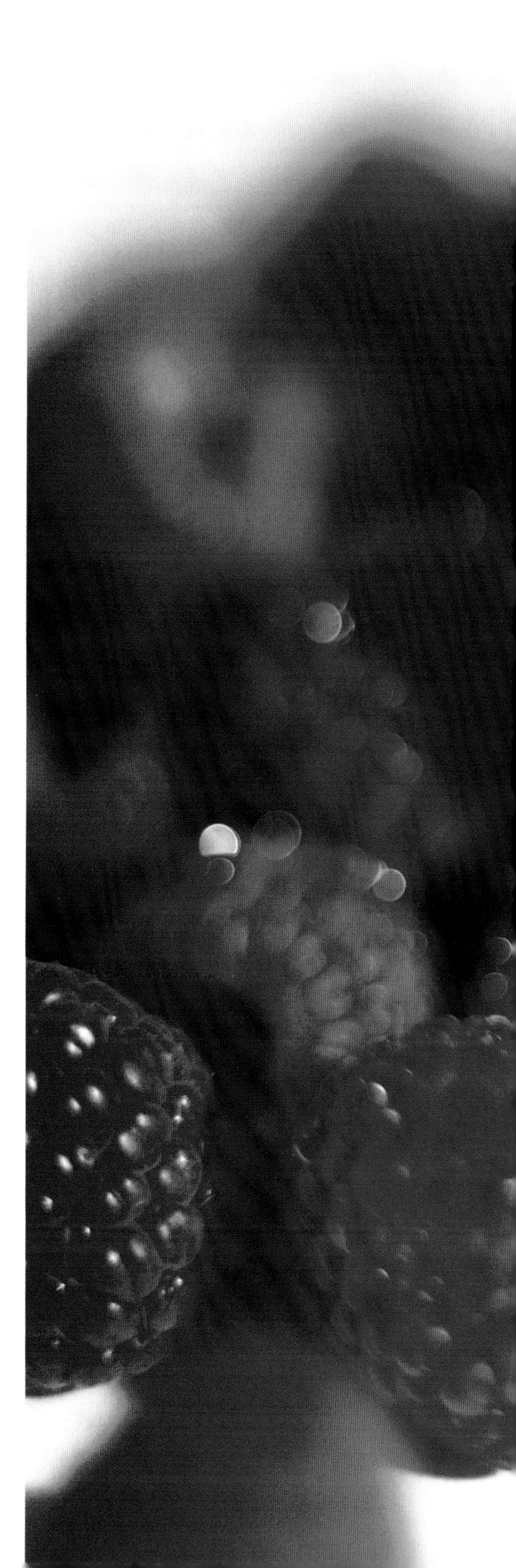

TEMPRANILLO

Tempranillo is important for the role it plays in many top-class Spanish red wines. Wines are of middle-weight in body with a juicy structure in their youth and some attractive strawberry flavours. The best wines age well and will gain a silky texture and beautiful spicy flavours. Ribera Del Duero and Rioja are the two most famous Tempranillo wines, those from Ribera tending to be firmer than those from Rioja.

ZINFANDEL

'Made' in the USA. Now that Californian growers treat this grape with respect some stunning wines are made with it: rich, round and concentrated with wonderful flavours of plum, blackberry, spice and raisin. The best examples will unquestionably improve with age. It is also widely used for the production of light and slightly sweet quaffing rosé wines.

other interesting red grapes

SANGIOVESE

The main grape used for Chianti. Producing middle-weight wines with a tight structure and characteristically stony and bitter cherry flavours. Capable of producing wines of great character and ageing potential by itself, it also blends well with Cabernet Sauvignon.

PINOTAGE

The grape of South Africa. Usually its wines are made in a light style, with some strange aromas of banana and sweet/sour fruit, to be drunk young. However, as more growers have started to take it seriously they are producing wines that can age, with more body and some appealing plummy and spicy flavours.

GRENACHE

Known as Garnacha in Spain where it is widely planted and used to produce superb red wines in the Priorato region, it is also used to produce very good wines in the Barossa Valley of Australia. It is most famous however for its leading role in the wine of Châteauneuf-du-Pape in the southern Rhône. Grenache produces wines that are sometimes light in colour, and have a round, smooth structure with black fruit, peppery and meaty flavours. Also greatly used for the production of rosé wines.

CABERNET FRANC

Cabernet Sauvignon's little brother. Normally blended with Cabernet Sauvignon and Merlot, and almost never used as the principal component of the blend (Bordeaux), it nevertheless has the leading role in the red wines of the Anjou and Touraine regions of France (Saumur, Bourgueil, Chinon). New World areas have now started producing some wines predominantly made from Cabernet Franc, which are lighter with green pepper and strawberry flavours.

MOURVEDRE

Planted in the wine area of Provence (Bandol) in France, in Spain under the name Monastrell and also in Australia and California as Mataro. Gives full-bodied wines with a firm structure and spicy and blackberry flavours.

MALBEC

Associated with the wines from the Cahors area in south-west France, but it gives its best results in Argentina. It produces relatively full-bodied wines with flavours that are difficult to define but which recall spice and black fruit.

CARMENERE

Widely planted in Chile, but often confused with Merlot. It produces wines with a deep colour, fairly full body and a round structure with some mulberry and spicy flavours.

BARBERA

Widely planted in Italy, it gives middle-weight wines with a fairly tight structure because of its high acidity. The flavours are difficult to define, but are rather like bitter fruit.

I could have included several more grape varieties but I simply wanted to give a quick overview of grapes that are both popular and have an interesting character. Bear in mind that the world of wine is not static, and a grape not planted in a particular area today could easily become its best asset tomorrow. The classic illustration of that point is of course New Zealand. In the early 1970s there were few Sauvignon Blancs from that area, but by the mid-1980s the grape had put New Zealand on the map of the great wine-producing countries.

chapter 3

tasting mechanisms

Wine-tasting is an activity that is performed with our sensory organs, using the senses of sight, smell, taste and touch. In fact in some professional circles it is referred to as either 'sensory evaluation of wine' or 'organoleptic evaluation of wine'. By following a technique using our senses, we will be able to evaluate a glass of wine and interpret our findings. Since our senses play such a fundamental role in wine-tasting, it is useful to have a basic understanding of how they function. In an extremely simplified manner, during wine-tasting a physical or chemical agent (called a stimulus) goes through one of our organs and reaches a receptor where some nerve cells (neurons) send a signal to the brain to be interpreted (see table opposite).

SIGHT

The sense of sight enables us to evaluate the appearance of a wine. Our eyes transmit messages to the brain, which will then interpret them in terms of hue and intensity of colour, clarity, brilliance, effervescence, fluidity/viscosity, and any other factors that can be detected visually. It is important not to forget that our visual judgement will be affected by our environment and the quality of the lighting.

the senses

SMELL

The sense of smell gives us the ability to appreciate the odour molecules of a wine, which are volatile or, in other words, a gas. These molecules are collected in two ways. The first is through our nose, via the nasal passage. The second is through our mouth, but in fact the molecules reach the same place, the olfactory bulb situated in the top part of the nasal cavities, only this time they are using the path at the back of the palate leading up to the nasal cavities. This second way is called the retro-nasal passage, and in effect it facilitates a passive smelling action. Both passages are very important because the sensation perceived is not exactly the same. By the second route the wine is warmed up in our mouth, releasing new molecules and

HOW THE SENSES WORK

	Sight	**Smell (nasal passage)**	**Smell (retro-nasal passage)**	**Taste**	**Touch**
Stimuli	Light waves	Odour molecules (in gas state)	Odour molecules (in gas state)	Sapid substances	Sapid substances
Organ attractor	Eyes	Nose	Mouth	Tongue	Palate
Receptor	Retina	Olfactory bulb	Olfactory bulb	Tastebuds	Trigeminal nerve endings
Conductor	Neurons	Neurons	Neurons	Neurons	Neurons
Interpreter	Brain	Brain	Brain	Brain	Brain

thus producing some slightly different sensations.

Memory plays an important role in wine-tasting, especially with regard to our perception of smells. Smells trigger recognition in our memory which allow them to be identified.

Our brain adapts to a smell very quickly, making it almost disappear. A typical example is being in a room with a strong smell, such as new paint or bleach – another person entering the room will be extremely conscious of it. One possible explanation of our ability to accustom ourselves to unpleasant smells so quickly is the idea that it gives us protection from that smell.

TASTE

The sense of taste supposedly only involves our perception of the four primary tastes: sweetness, sourness (which has a negative connotation for wine so we talk of it as acidity; indeed a wine turning sour becomes vinegar), bitterness and saltiness (not very important in wine). Found in the different types of papillae on the tongue, taste buds are the receptors of our sense of taste.

Research into our senses is under way all over the world, for they are still not fully understood. For instance Professor Linda Bartoshuk of Yale University of Medicine in New Haven, Connecticut, as reported by Clive Cookson in the *Financial Times*: 'The Nature of Things', and Tim Atkin in *Wine,* March 1998, has done research on the reaction in the mouth to a synthetic chemical called 6-n-propylthiouracil, or Prop, to give some indication as to the tasting abilities of the people tested. Approximately 25 per cent of the population would be super tasters, the majority of them women, 50 per cent would be normal tasters and 25 per cent non-tasters. The research has shown that the higher the concentration of taste buds on the tongue, the better the sense of taste. However this test relies solely on taste buds and ignores our senses of smell and touch, which, although correct when assessing taste proper, can be misleading in relation to the more general sense of taste.

At the same university, Dr Alberto Cruz and Dr Barry Green, as reported by Nick Nuttall in *The Times* in 1999, have conducted tests demonstrating that the temperature at which food is served can alter a person's perception of whether it is sweet, sour, salty or bitter.

The long-held belief that there are only four primary tastes detectable on the tongue has been challenged by some eminent scientists. A fifth taste sensation which is called Umami (discovered by Professor K. Ikeda and announced in 1912), and is linked with glutamate (found, for example, in soy sauce), has started to be recognised by professional tasters such as E. Peynaud in *The Taste of Wine.*

A leading French neuroscientist, Dr Annick Faurion, is not alone in thinking that our tongue is capable of

sensing much more than the four classic primary tastes. Dr Faurion explains that it is for convenience, a sort of mental laziness, that we have kept only four basic references in our vocabulary of taste. She argues that we should think more in terms of a continuum of tastes perceived on the tongue. After all, sweetness is not a single unique sensation.

Professional tasters find it difficult to move away from the simple and traditional concept of four or five definitive sensations. An analogy lies in the world of politics. When we classify a mainstream politician in the UK we think of only three possible definitions: Labour on the left; Liberal Democrat in the centre; and Conservative on the right. However we know that more tendencies exist: in the Labour Party: some are on the right of the party, some are in the centre and some are on the left of the party, and this is also true of the other two parties resulting in an abundance of possibilities as is the case with taste sensations.

Dr Faurion also refutes the conventional idea that there are some preferential zones on the tongue such as sweet on the tip or saltiness on the side. In wine, as in many other fields, we need some simple reference points to guide our understanding and appraisal and to avoid the confusion of a multitude of references. However we must never forget that a framework is never the complete picture.

TOUCH

With regard to wine-tasting, the sense of touch relates to tactile, thermal and chemical sensations. It enables us to evaluate, among other things, the weight, consistency, astringency, temperature, and the effects of carbon dioxide and sulphur dioxide in a wine. The trigeminal nerve, found in the face, skin and mucosae, plays an important role in the transmission of some of these sensations to the brain.

The conventional way to taste a wine is to pour a sample of it into a glass (filled to a third; see page 17), look at it, smell it and then take a small sample in the mouth; finally, based on all the observations, draw your overall conclusion. The process falls into four distinct sections: appearance – the wine's visual impression; nose – the wine's odours; palate – the wine's flavours, structures and aftertaste; and conclusion – an overall evaluation and interpretation of the wine. Each section is further divided into precise subsections which are explained in the pages that follow.

Within each section, it is not essential to tackle the appraisal in the order I suggest. However, once you have established your own order within each section do stick to it. By doing so, it will quickly become second nature to you, and you will have less chance of forgetting any fundamental aspect.

As you study a wine, record all the information you can, as it is from these notes that you will form your final judgement. The more information you gather about the wine you are tasting, the more precise your conclusion will be. For each subsection I give a list (or lists) of the most commonly used words to describe the observations. In sommelier competitions candidates are often asked to recount, in front of an audience, a complete description of a particular wine; suggestions for the most appropriate descriptions are given in each paragraph.

tasting techniques

As mentioned, fill the tasting glass to a third of its volume; holding it by the stem, tilt it slightly in front of a white background. Tilting the glass gives you a larger wine surface to help you to evaluate the difference in colour between the core and the edge, and it gives you a better idea of its intensity of colour. While most of the observation is done with the glass slightly tilted, to assess the wine's brilliance the glass should be held perfectly straight and the wine looked at from directly above.

Observations in this section cover:

CLARITY

BRILLIANCE

COLOUR

CARBON DIOXIDE

CONSISTENCY, FLUIDITY/VISCOSITY

Many of these are interrelated, but to be thorough it is important to differentiate between them. For instance the brilliance of a wine will partly depend on its clarity, but not every clear wine is brilliant.

CLARITY

A finished wine should be free of visible impurities. It should not look murky. Some unfiltered wines might not look as clear as the great majority of wines, but even so they should not be hazy. Of course if you taste wine directly from the vat or the cask a touch of haze is almost inevitable. An old bottle of wine could have some natural sediment, so ensure that none remains in the wine when assessing it. Either decant the bottle carefully before tasting or simply pour it very gently.

White and rosé wine: limpid, clear for the slightly darker ones.

Red wine: limpid for the very light-coloured ones, clear for most of them, opaque for very deeply saturated ones.

Negative description (any colour): cloudy, hazy, murky.

BRILLIANCE

The pH (measure of acid concentration) also influences the colour of a wine; the more acid the wine (with a low pH), the more brilliant its colour. The level of brilliance also depends on the handling of the wine during maturation. Wines that have been cold stabilised, fined and tightly filtered will be more

appearance

brilliant than those that have been less manipulated. Nevertheless a wine should not be dull – even a very opaque red wine. If it is, it is a sign of deterioration.

White, rosé and red wine: star bright, then brilliant and bright. Differences hardly exist between them but personally I like to use star bright for very bright whites to accentuate their level of brilliance.

Negative: dull.

COLOUR

The colour of a wine is determined principally by climate, grape variety, maturity of the grape, wine-making methods and maturity of the wine.

Cooler climates tend to produce wines lighter in colour, while warmer ones produce darker colours.

Grape variety is less important for white wines, although some grapes (such as Gewürztraminer) do give a fuller colour. For rosé and red wines it is a major factor as some varieties have more colouring pigments in the skins of their berries. Cabernet Sauvignon and Shiraz both give very dark red wines, whereas Pinot Noir generally gives a lighter colour.

The maturity of the grapes has an obvious effect: the riper the grapes the stronger the colour.

In the making of white wine, cold temperatures and maturation in stainless steel give a lighter colour; oak ageing tends to give deeper colours because of the greater oxidation, although some very old oak vats, through having contained many wines, have become so airtight that little oxidation occurs. In the making of rosé and red wines the more extracted from the skins during fermentation and the longer the skins remain in contact with the juice, the fuller the colour. A very long maturation time (three to five years or more) in wooden barrels accelerates the loss of colour.

In sweet wines, the more desiccated the berries (by botrytis or slow drying) the darker the colour, and in fortified wines less contact with oxygen produces a lighter colour; more contact, a darker colour.

In terms of maturity, in a white wine, the younger the wine the lighter the colour; the older the darker (due to oxidation). In a rosé or red wine, the younger the wine the deeper the colour; the older the lighter (the slow deposit of colouring pigments and tannin compounds during ageing cause it to lose colour).

Hue

White wine: a white wine starts with a greenish yellow colour and develops up to a more brownish yellow (by which stage it is almost dead).

Hues in order of evolution: watery, pale yellow, green yellow, lemon yellow, young gold, old gold, brownish.

Rosé wine: the hue for a rosé wine is not so marked by ageing (simply because they tend to be consumed in their youth) but more by grape variety and vinification process.

Hues in order of style, from fresh to full: raspberry, strawberry, pomegranate, salmon, apricot.

Red wine: a red wine starts with a purple hue and develops to a brown at the very end of its existence. *Hues in order of evolution*: purple, ruby, redcurrant, garnet, cherry, orangey red, brick or tile, tawny, brown.

Fortified and some sweet wine: it is difficult to generalise about the hue of fortified and sweet wine as so many wine-making techniques are used. Also their life expectancy is far greater than that of other types of wine. Some Madeira wines or old vintage ports, for instance, can be drunk when they are more than fifty years old. So, in addition to the colours for white, rosé and red wines, here are a few more: copper, bronze, terracotta, chestnut, walnut, prune, greenish brown.

Variation

It is especially important for this exercise that you look at the glass when it is tilted at an angle. The colour of the wine will either show a slightly different shade at the edge of the glass, referred to as rim variation, or reflections of a slightly different colour will appear in the body of the wine, referred to as tinges. Because red wines have a fuller colour than white ones, they present more variation in their colour (being deeper in the centre); rim is therefore more relevant, while tinges are more relevant to white wines due to their greater clarity and brilliance. Both rim (paler) and tinges (more

brilliant) are an indication of a wine's maturity: the more accentuated the rim or tinge the more evolved the wine will be.

Rim for red wine in order of evolution: violet, pink, cherry, garnet, tile, tawny, brown. You can also use shades given for the hue, but don't over-complicate. You cannot use the same colour for both the rim and the hue, as that would mean there was no variation.

Tinges for white wine in order of evolution: silver, green, straw, golden, bronze. You could use the shades given under hue, but again keep it simple. Tinges can be so powerful that they can be seen as part of the hue, as in green yellow.

Intensity

The intensity of the wine's colour provides a lot of information, giving clues as to climate, grape variety (principally for red wines) and ripeness, vinification method, age and maturity.

White/rosé wine: pale, light, medium, medium-full, full.

Red wine: light, medium, medium-full, full, dense, opaque.

Some descriptions of colour already incorporate a wine's intensity, as in pale yellow, so there is no point in repeating the information by saying that a pale yellow white wine has a pale intensity. In this instance simply make no note or refer back to colour.

CARBON DIOXIDE

Every wine contains some CO_2 but in most still wines the level is normally low enough not to be visible. However in some very young wines, often those to be drunk in their youth, the level can be slightly higher because a bit more gas has been deliberately retained from the fermentation or a small amount may have been added to give a fresher feel to the wine and so bubbles will be apparent. It is also possible, but not common nowadays, that a bottle may have a refermentation problem, in which case not only the bubbles will be visible, but the lees of this second fermentation will give a slightly hazy look to the wine. Sparkling wine, of course, has plenty of CO_2.

In still wine, look for the absence or presence of CO_2. If there are bubbles, note their quantity and size; in other words whether there are many or few bubbles and how large or small they are.

In sparkling wine look for the quantity of bubbles, their size, their speed of formation and duration.

Presence of CO_2; None visible or presence of a small or a large quantity of minute, medium or big bubbles (pearls) of CO_2; rising quickly, fairly quickly, very quickly; remaining for a short time or for a long time.

A good sparkling wine should have a fairly consistent ring of small bubbles at the rim of the glass, breaking gently, but reforming quickly in the regular arrival of a stream of new bubbles from the bottom of the glass. This is the theory, but in practice it does not always work like this. The glass itself may affect the bubbles. Using too much detergent when washing the glass can have a devastating effect on the quality of the foam, while a glass with a scratch inside at the bottom will produce more bubbles because the scratch gives an active point on which the bubbles can form. Older sparkling wines have less CO_2 through natural loss and therefore are less sparkling than when first made. So judging the quality of sparkle in a sparkling wine does not always provide a very accurate assessment of a wine's quality. That said, it is generally true that large bubbles and short duration of the ring of bubbles at the rim are indicators of lesser quality.

CONSISTENCY, FLUIDITY/VISCOSITY

The higher the amount of alcohol, residual sugar for wines other than dry ones, and colour and tannin for red wines, the fuller and more viscous the wine will be in appearance. These qualities are best observed by swirling the glass consistently and gently so that the wine rotates slowly. You can then decide if the wine looks very fluid, quite fluid, fairly viscous, or very viscous.

Some tasters refer to the tears (also called legs, arches or even cathedral windows in Germany) formed inside the glass and falling down slowly back into the wine after swirling, and note their thickness and speed of fall. Tears are formed because the difference in volatility between alcohol and water creates a higher surface tension on the rim of the glass, causing the liquid to rise and later drop back. The higher the alcohol level in the wine the more tears are visible. Once again however, the way the glass has been washed may affect their formation. Personally, I look at them for a first indication as to the level of alcohol, but I do not dwell on them at any length.

Having completed the first section of your study, it might be quite useful to draw up some first impressions as to climate, the maturity of the wine, the quality of the vintage, and so on, but be careful not to jump to any definite conclusions as yet.

For this section, make sure you treat each wine in the same manner, smelling each for the same length of time; such consistency means that the wines can be judged more accurately. I like to smell a wine two or three times fairly briefly at first, then after a break return to it for one single longer smell to discover new aromas. To get the maximum from the smell of a wine you need to swirl the glass before you nose it. This will increase the release of odour molecules and give you more information on the smell of the wine. It also explains why the glass must be narrow at the top and not filled to more than a third. It is not very difficult to do, but nevertheless to avoid red wine on the carpet I suggest you start practising in the bathroom or in the garden with water rather than wine until you feel confident. An easy way to get used to the swirling movement is to put your glass on a table and rotate it slowly while keeping it firmly on the table.

Observations in this section cover:

CONDITION

INTENSITY

CHARACTER

nose

CONDITION

When starting to smell the wine, the first aspect to focus your mind on is its condition; in other words whether the wine is sound to drink or not. Cork taint is the most common source of complaints, but other faults do exist (see the section on faults in chapter 4 pages 96–9). Some wines may not be exactly faulty but, none the less, have a rather strange smell.

Positive: (and how every bottle should be) clean.
Questioning: strange, curious, dubious.
Negative: faulty.

INTENSITY

The difference in the strength of the smell between wines is quite astonishing; some wines have hardly any aroma, while others almost overpower you. One of the principal reasons for this is the grape variety from which the wine is made. Other factors can play a role, for instance a slightly higher than normal level of carbon dioxide in a still wine will increase the strength of its smell, giving it a fresher nose.

Smell in order of strength: close, weak, moderately open, quite open, open, powerful, extremely powerful.

It is important to note that a wine does not need to have a powerful nose to be a great wine. It is also the case that some very good wines go through a 'dumb' period when they smell very little, but after a few years start to develop a wonderful bouquet.

CHARACTER

Here we look at the main families of smells (fruit, floral, animal, mineral, etc.) and to which groups of wines they tend to belong. Remember that a smell can only be perceived if the odorous compound is volatile (a gas). In the appendix on pages 180–3 the main elements that compose a wine are explained in relation to their role in taste.

Many wine smells have been isolated in single chemical compounds (such as aldehydes or esters) that are also found in other products. We could, of course, refer to them by their chemical name which is often what oenologists do, but that would be complicated, confusing and frankly pretentious outside a laboratory. And, of course, if you use the chemical name for one component you have to do it for all of them. You could not say for instance that a wine has an appealing methoxypyrazines (herbaceous) smell while another smelling of melon is rather disappointing.

Wine smells can originate directly from the grapes or the climatic conditions, form during the vinification and/or maturation of the wine or develop during the ageing process.

Grape smells are found in wines made from aromatic grapes, but only when the wines are young; later other smells take over (and aromatic grapes can lose their identity under the influence of some wine-making techniques, such as the use of new oak). Young aromatic wines tend to smell of fresh fruit (apple, passion fruit, apricot) and fresh flowers (rose, violet).

Climatic conditions will of course play a role in the creation of a wine's smell. Wines made from grapes grown in cool climatic conditions will have a 'greener' smell (apple, herbaceous, wild berry) than those grown in warmer conditions (tropical fruit, plum, raisin). In addition, the timing of the harvest can produce a similar effect: early as for cool climate, late as for warm.

Vinification and maturation smells are found in wines that are made from less aromatic grapes and where the vinification process has a strong influence on the smell of the wine. As we have seen in the last chapter, carbonic maceration, flavour-enhancing yeasts, cold fermentation, maturation in new oak, malolactic fermentation, flor maturation, oxidative maturation and lee maturation are all wine-making techniques that have a great influence on the smell of the wine.

Ageing or development smells take over from the other groups of smells after a certain period, although exactly when is not clear: in some wines it can take place after only five years, in others not until ten or more. It is important to note that only a very limited number of wines benefit from this transformation. Those wines that age gracefully will be categorised into two very distinct families: one called reductive and the other oxidative. The first one (reductive ageing) concerns most of the classic still red or white wines. Normally these wines are bottled between anything from one to two years after fermentation, which means that if they are drunk when ten, twenty or more years of age, most of their ageing will have been in bottles away from oxygen. In those conditions wines develop some wonderful smells, often animal (game, leather), vegetal (moss, truffle), wood (cedar) and others, harder to group together, such as chocolate or tobacco. I need to point out that some types of reductive smells can start much earlier in the winery if the wines, especially red ones, do not get enough oxygen contact. In some cases the wine can smell very unpleasant, overly gamey, and it can develop to become even worse (see Hydrogen Sulphide in wine faults in chapter 4 page 98). However, a very little reductive ageing in a young red wine can be perfectly acceptable, although young reductive smells never have the finesse of those born from long ageing in the bottle.

The second family is that of oxidative ageing, which simply means wines that have been made with an oxidative maturation (see chapter 2 page 40). These wines have often been matured for many years (five, ten or more) in wood casks and have been submitted to a slow and controlled oxygen intake before bottling. As mentioned earlier, this technique is used principally for some kinds of fortified wines; expect to find nut, toffee, caramel, nutmeg and wood polish in their smells.

At this point it is worth explaining that you will hear some tasters referring to aroma and others to bouquet. Technically speaking, aroma refers to the smell of young wine, while bouquet refers to the more complex smell of older wine. To confuse matters further, oenologists now talk of odour for the nose and mouth aroma for the palate.

Some tasters would argue that there is another factor that is the source of many wonderful and unique smells. They are referring to those originating from the *terroir*, or specific location where the grapes were grown, with its combination of soil, site and climate. Whereas the effects of climatic conditions alone on smells are relatively obvious, when site and soil are added in to the equation it all becomes much more difficult to understand. Nevertheless there is no doubt that some areas produce wines with truly inimitable smells that can be justified neither by climatic conditions alone nor by grape, wine-making or ageing. In my opinion, the *terroir* factor cannot be isolated

Although looking at the individual components is useful, it is important to be aware that each is affected by the others. For instance, the sensation given by acidity can be masked by sweetness. In effect they are all quite interdependent.

SUGAR

The greater the amount of residual sugar left in the wine the sweeter it will be. Nevertheless, the sensation of sweetness can be diminished by high levels of acidity or, conversely, increased by low levels of acidity. Sweetness is a soft, smooth, mellow sensation that most people, especially pudding lovers, understand very well. If in any doubt try a spoonful of honey or suck a caramel.

In order of sweetness: bone dry, dry, off-dry, medium dry, medium sweet, sweet, very sweet.

ACIDITY

The higher the level of acidity and the lower the amount of residual sugar left in the wine, the stronger the sensation of acidity will be. Acidity provides a fresh, crisp feeling on the tongue. However, sometimes people confuse acid and bitter sensations. Bite into a fresh lemon or grapefruit to feel acidity and drink a strong coffee or a tonic water to experience bitterness.

In order of increasing acidity: low, moderate, reasonable, marked, high.

ALCOHOL

The taste of alcohol is difficult to define precisely, but it provides a slightly sweet taste and at a high level it produces a warm, almost burning, sensation. Mix a measure of unflavoured vodka at 40 per cent of alcohol in two measures of water and taste it to feel the sweetish sensation; then try a mixture of one measure of vodka and one measure of water to experience the warm sensation of a higher level of alcohol.

In order of increasing alcohol: low, moderate, noticeable, high.

TANNIN

Since tannins are principally extracted from the skins and the stems of the grapes, the tannic sensation mainly concerns red wines. However, oak maturation does impart some wood tannin so white wines aged in new oak have more tannin than those matured in stainless steel, although never nearly as much as a red wine made in the traditional manner. Tannin produces a drying and puckering effect on the palate, referred to as astringency, which gives an impression of hardness in the mouth. Again it should not be confused with bitterness, although unripe tannins will also add some bitterness to the astringent sensation. The strength of its effect is chiefly linked with the level of tannin in the fruit, the amount extracted during fermentation and the evolution of the wine (during ageing tannins slowly transform and eventually precipitate to the bottom). To experience a strong tannic sensation, put two teabags in a mug and let them infuse for a while; compare its taste with that of a mug of tea made of one teabag infused for a very short time.

In order of increasing tannin: weak (negative), soft, smooth, firm, rough (negative).

Firmer tannins, as long as these are not rough, are acceptable and often expected in a young red wine; although a young red wine does not have to have firm tannins to be good.

CARBON DIOXIDE

Still wines do contain some carbon dioxide, but in most cases the level is low enough not to be noticeable on the palate. However if the CO_2 was removed from the wine, it would taste flat. In fact, a small amount of CO_2 is deliberately added to some young, fresh styles of wines to enhance their structure. The sensation on the palate given by CO_2 is not too dissimilar to that given by acidity.

In still wines in which CO_2 *is noticeable, in increasing order*: refreshing, zesty, spritzig, prickling (a touch negative for a still wine).

In sparkling wines the sensation will be either very fresh, as in many young examples, or much softer in more mature examples.

In young sparkling wine: refreshing, youthful, zingy, green (negative), but you can also use some terms more usually applied to acidity, such as crisp or fresh.

In mature sparkling wines: there are few words to describe the gentle sparkle sensation provided: slightly creamy, quite creamy, very creamy.

BODY

This is the impression of weight the wine gives in the mouth. It comes from the alcohol and the non-volatile wine constituents (fixed acids, phenolics, minerals, glycerol and residual sugars) grouped under the term extract. If it seems strange to talk of the weight of wine, compare the different weight impressions given when drinking full-cream milk as opposed to half-fat or low-fat milk.

In order of increasing body: thin, light, middle-weight, full-bodied, heavy.

STRUCTURE/TEXTURE

The structure of a wine is not easy to define, but it can be interpreted as a combination of a wine's body and texture. The texture of wine itself comes from the combination of the amount or quality of the residual sugar, acidity, alcohol and tannin. In addition, by its impact on the palate, the concentration of flavour will also play a part in shaping a wine's structure.

All sorts of words have been used to describe a wine's structure. Using some of the most common from the language of wine I have divided this section into seven families. To each I have added a couple of words that can be used either as a synonym for or complement to the family heading, usually with one referring specifically to white wine and the other to red wine. Two of these families describe a negative impression and five a positive one.

Coarse: a negative description for wines having a poor structure dominated either by acidity (sharp) or by tannin (hard). In the same vein are wines that have lost their flavours and are left with mainly acidity or tannin (dried out).

Solid: a positive description for full-bodied wines with an excellent structure but with either a dominant acidity as in some white wines (steely) or some firm but ripe tannins (robust).

Tight: a positive description for lighter wines than the previous family, also with an excellent structure but again with either a dominant acidity (crisp) or firm/ripe tannins (close-knit).

Juicy: a positive description for wines dominated neither by acidity nor tannin, which nevertheless convey a feeling of beneficial vigour, albeit in a different way. In this family, I include the more youthful wines dominated by the exuberance of their fruit flavours, both white (fresh) and red wines (lively).

Supple: a positive description for light- or middle-weight wines producing a gentle feeling in the mouth thanks to a sufficient level of perfectly integrated acidity (delicate) or tannin (silky) supporting the wines imperceptibly.

Round: a positive description for full-bodied wines with great texture and no hard edges, either white (fat) or red (velvety).

Flat: a negative description for wines with a poor structure largely due to an insufficient level of acidity (flabby), sometimes accentuated by far too much residual sugar in relation to the acidity (cloying). The term flat can also be applied to sparkling wines, and, on rare occasions, still wines, with insufficient CO_2.

Of course there are other words that are perfectly adequate to describe a wine's structure: harsh, green, tough, chewy, austere, severe and loose on the negative side, and rich, luscious, mellow, fleshy, ample, compact or even some of those used for the other sections: soft, smooth, firm, zingy and creamy on the positive side.

FLAVOURS

For a full definition of the word flavour, see my system in chapter 5 pages 127–35. Here it is used to designate only the smells felt in the mouth by the retro-nasal passage.

The smells detected should be similar to those found on the nose with perhaps some variations on account of the fact that the wine has warmed up in the palate. We will look at their character and concentration.

The characters of flavours in the mouth are similar to (or confirm) the smells found on the nose (see earlier nose section pages 68–72). As the wine warms up on the palate new smells emerge, usually less powerful ones, so in the description the taster might say: 'Confirm the nose with tropical fruit and hints of aniseed.'

In order of concentration: weak, moderate, filling the palate well, packed.

BALANCE

A wine can give an impression of harmony because all the elements fit together or, conversely, it can seem not to combine very well. (See balance in chapter 4 pages 94–5.)

The wine therefore can be well balanced, balanced but with dominant acidity, or tannins, etc., or unbalanced because of its high alcohol or low acidity.

LENGTH

The length is important in determining the overall quality of the wine (see definition in chapter 4 page 95). Some tasters define the quality of the length by timing it exactly. They count the time in caudalies (1 caudalie = 1 second of flavour remaining once the wine has been spat out or swallowed) and they call this the PAI from the French: *Persistance Aromatic Intense*. I find this method extremely unreliable, as so many factors interact on the aftertaste: the initial amount of wine in the mouth, the taster's breathing, confusion between tastes (acid, bitter, sweet, salt, umami) and flavours, as well as the effects of mental tiredness. I agree entirely with Professor Peynaud who says in his book *The Taste Of Wine*: 'This method [counting in caudalies] has the advantage of demanding a careful analysis when tasting, but it can be criticized for being too rigid and for implying a precision which does not exist.' It is impossible to be so accurate, and while length of flavour is important, so is its quality. I prefer to limit myself to see if the wine has: an unpleasant finish, an indifferent finish, a nice finish, or a beautiful and long finish.

conclusion

We are at the final round-up and we have to give a reasoned assessment. If we knew the type and style of the wines, but not the names of the estates and were asked to comment on their quality, we might talk of:

State of maturity: immature, mature.

Development: backward (late in development), developing well, forward (too advanced for its age).

Potential: drink now, drink or keep (within three to five years), keep (ten years or more), past it.

Typicity: typical, moderately typical, untypical.

Ripeness: unripe, slightly unripe, nicely ripe, very ripe.

Quality: faulty, inferior, average, superior, outstanding.

Value for money: poor, modest, fair, excellent, fabulous.

Food suggestion: would suit foods that are spicy, mild, simple, sophisticated, then suggest some dishes.

Optimal drinking temperature: thinking of the ambient temperature (e.g. summer, winter) 8–18°C (46–64°F).

If we knew nothing about the wines and we were asked to identify them, we would consider:

Flavour and style: wine type (character), varietal type (flavours of grape), wine-making method (flavours of vinification and maturation), combination of flavours (flavours of both and more: *terroir*?).

Ageing method: reductive (protected from oxygen), oxidative (controlled oxidation).

Orientation: mass market, mid market, premium market.

Quality: faulty, inferior, average, superior, outstanding.

Verdict: grape(s), country, region, vintage.

chapter 4

quality in wine

Quality is arguably the single most important factor in a wine-buying decision. Quite naturally, we all want the best quality within any price bracket or style category. But while the desire for quality is understandable, what constitutes quality in wine is much more difficult to appreciate.

Even the word quality is confusing. It can be understood in the sense of a specific property as in, 'the most obvious quality of this wine is its high alcohol level', or it can be used to designate superiority as in 'this is the best quality Chardonnay I have tasted from that area'. It is, of course, in the sense of excellence that I will try to explain quality in wine; and it is with absolute quality that I am concerned. First of all let us reflect on several elements connected, rightly or wrongly, with the idea of quality and see, when assessing a glass of wine, if they play any sort of role.

PERSONAL TASTE

Wine books and guides, perhaps partly to reassure the reader or gain their support, sometimes vaguely declare that the important thing is that you know what you like and that you should not pay too much attention to

ALBOT
12 Btles
DOMAINES CORDIER
CHATEAU TALBOT

the extensive advice available wherever you turn. Of course no one can tell you what you like, and it is not my intention to do so either, but that does not mean that personal preferences are related to quality. Some wine drinkers enjoy the strong toasty-vanilla flavour that new oak gives to wine, but a wine dominated by this type of taste is not a wine of high quality, even if I do admit to having occasionally enjoyed such wines myself. To be regarded as having any real quality, a wine should smell and taste of much more than just new oak. It is, after all, made of grapes.

REPUTATION

If you were contemplating buying a few cases for laying down, would you rather buy the wine from an estate with a good track record or from a little-known property? It seems perfectly logical to opt for the wine with the strongest reputation. In general, good reputations are built up over the years thanks to consistency in the quality of their production. Nevertheless, past performances are no guarantee of the quality of today's wine. Even top domaines do underachieve on occasion. It is an open secret that

Château Margaux did not always live up to its great reputation before it was bought by the Mentzelopoulos family in 1977! This is a famous example, but I could easily have named other renowned wineries that have been through difficult patches. In effect, reputation is rather like checking the form of a horse before placing a bet on it, but knowing full well that its form, no matter how good, is no guarantee for the next race. Similarly when you are assessing a wine, reputation is of no relevance.

TRENDS

Trends are not the same as reputation, but the effects are not dissimilar. The wines from a particular area or grape variety can suddenly become very fashionable, which may then give the impression that they must be of good quality. After all, the idea that if it is popular it must be good is not illogical. Why would so many people buy a product if did not have a real element of quality? Well, as we know, it does not always work like that. Indeed the theory can easily be demolished,

especially in the wine trade, simply by remembering certain famous brands that have enjoyed tremendous popularity at one stage, thanks more to their clever marketing than to any real quality.

And even if the trend does hit on a perfectly valid level of quality, there will be enormous variation within it. For instance, Chilean wines are fairly fashionable at present, often deservedly so, and the same can be said of wines made from the Viognier grape; nevertheless, not every bottle of Chilean wine, nor every Viognier wine will be of great quality. As with reputation, trend plays no part in the tasting room.

RARITY

Rarity is another attribute that can affect our perception of a wine's real quality. Small is beautiful! In the wine trade there is often a sense that wines made by small estates (often referred to as 'boutique' wineries) are automatically better than those made by much larger companies. The romantic idea that if you produce less you will have more time and more control over what goes on in the vineyard and the winery is quite understandable, and in many cases it is true that more care is given by owners of small wineries to their wines. However, there are also many examples of substandard wines made in small wineries as a result of a lack of technical competence and necessary equipment, and there are plenty of well-run large estates consistently delivering outstanding wines. Antinori in Italy, Beringer in California, Jadot in Burgundy and Brown Brothers in Australia are just a few examples of large wineries that regularly produce delicious wines.

The wine in your glass might be rare, but that doesn't necessarily make it better.

PRICE

In the absence of any other information, price will be used as an indication of quality. If it is expensive then it must be good! A simple deduction, which we have all been guilty of making, whether consciously or subconsciously. Yes, even wine experts do occasionally fall for this. They might not apply this reasoning to wine, but away from their field of expertise they fall back on this erroneous assumption.

Price and quality, as with so many things in life, must be related. To a certain extent you get what you pay for. Thanks to today's technological advances in wine-making and the improved grape quality from very warm climates it is possible to produce large quantities of fairly enjoyable wines at a reasonable price, but rarely do those wines truly excite. Wineries cannot perform miracles. To produce outstanding wines, high-quality grapes are needed, which because of the time and attention that are devoted to them in the vineyard, will cost more than those produced in a more industrial fashion. Wineries might not need state-of-the-art equipment but they still have to purchase quality materials, such as new oak barrels. Furthermore, talented wine-makers live in the real world and command high salaries. All these factors logically have a larger or smaller part to play in the price of the final bottle.

While reputation, trends and rarity are not relevant when assessing quality, they indubitably come into the price equation to distort a wine's true value. You just need to look at some of the wine prices found in the catalogues of famous wine-brokers to understand what reputation, trends and rarity can do for an estate. In fact the chances of being listed if the winery has none of these attributes are very remote. The best illustration is provided by the new breed of estates: 'Les Garagistes' (so-called because of their small size; they could almost make their wine in garages). The wines of these estates, though often of excellent quality, sell at much higher prices than their true value, principally because of their scarcity and their extremely fashionable image. I would readily drink and enjoy many of the wines found on these lists, but to say that their price is an accurate reflection of their quality is quite another matter. At the top level, prices often increase faster than quality.

When appraising a glass of wine, pay no attention to its price because it is not a sound criterion for quality.

VALUE FOR MONEY

Imagine you and I tasted two wines, A and B, and we thought that wine A was marginally better, so we rated them as wine A 16 points and wine B 15.5 points. When we discovered that wine B was half the price of wine A, would wine B become a better wine than wine A? If we are talking absolute quality, of course not!

I do know of some tasters who alter the final mark

they give to a wine after discovering its price. Although to do so arises from a commendable spirit, it is in my opinion quite wrong. Value for money does not play a part in evaluating quality, but rather the reverse.

The wine you are tasting might be great value but it is not inherently better for that.

TYPICITY (TYPICALNESS)

When buying anything, we expect it to conform to our expectations. If I asked for a pound of Cheddar in a shop and when I got home realised they had given me a pound of butter, I would be annoyed, but that does not make the butter of lesser quality. In fact the butter could be very good and the Cheddar might have been truly mediocre. It simply didn't fit the category I had specified.

In the same way, at some regional tastings, wines can be refused the nomenclature of that area on the grounds of not being in its typical style. This may be in terms of the wine's style or of the grapes used to make it, as was the case with Eloi Dürrbach of Domaine de Trévallon who was excluded from the Beaux-de-Provence appellation despite the quality of his wines

Although I do not think of typicalness as a mark of quality, I would be quite puzzled if when tasting a range of young Chablis wines I found one with a strong tropical character on the nose, instead of the more usual mineral/floral/appley/marzipan character.

Because of my knowledge of the different styles of wines, it would be difficult for me not to be unconsciously influenced one way or the other.

Nevertheless, the truth of the matter is that a wine is not better because it follows the expected style. It is simply conforming to type.

ABSENCE OF DEFECTS

An absence of defects seems a prerequisite for any wine even to begin to be considered as having any sort of quality. However, zero faults does not necessarily guarantee quality. Bear in mind those beautiful shiny red tomatoes, all of a similar shape and size, but in most cases tasteless.

Unfortunately in wine production a similar concept is not unusual. Some wine-makers, for instance, will go to great lengths to prevent the formation of harmless crystal tartrate, which can occur naturally in wine, as consumers often mistake the tartrate crystals for broken glass. While such wine-making treatments to avoid crystal tartrate might improve the appearance of the wine, they also reduce its flavour.

Indeed some wine-makers are more intent on producing wines without defects than wines of truly exciting character. To be fair, wine-makers involved in the production of mass-market wines do not always have a choice, as visible imperfections would lead to their exclusion from that market, no matter what the overall quality of the wines.

If you found no defects when appraising a wine, that simply means it is fit to drink, not that it has any sort of quality.

So far, every topic we have examined counts for very little when you are trying to assess the absolute quality of the wine in your glass. The significance of the next topic, potential, is much harder to determine.

POTENTIAL

For many wine lovers the potential of a wine to age is seen as a great quality. To be more accurate I should say improve rather than age. It is what differentiates wine from many other consumable goods. Nevertheless it is important to remember that only a very small percentage of wines do actually improve with age; some barely survive, while the great majority of wines deteriorate fairly quickly.

But when assessing a category of wines known for its ageing capabilities at an early stage, it is only natural that the tasters should try to foresee their future. Certainly it is a wonderful experience to drink older wines that have developed a unique character on the nose and a marvellous textural appeal. It is indeed a definite mark of quality if a wine can improve over many years.

But can only those wines capable of ageing be considered as of the best quality? Can the purity of aroma coupled with a fresh and juicy feel on the palate never match a complex smell with a smooth texture? A lamb stew is a beautiful dish that can be reheated the following day and taste even better, whereas a grilled Dover sole would taste terrible if reheated, but when eaten the instant it is ready is delicious. So is the stew a better food simply because it can improve? I have been fortunate enough to taste some old German Riesling to die for, but I have also experienced some truly exciting tastes with young Alsace Riesling from growers such as Marcel Deiss or Olivier Zind-Humbrecht MW.

There is no denying that great old wines are unique, but their image is also embellished by the fact that there are fewer of them. So in some small measure their attraction is increased by their rarity.

Yet many wines provide so much pleasure when young that there is little reason to be interested in their ageing potential. Most Sauvignon Blanc wines spring to mind. Are Cloudy Bay Sauvignon Blanc and a few other great Marlborough Sauvignon Blancs of lesser quality because they might not improve?

Attempting to judge both the pleasure a wine is giving now and the pleasure it will give in ten or twenty years' time is not an easy affair, and tasters do get it wrong. For instance, when tasted in their youth by several wine experts, most of the top red Bordeaux of the 1975 vintage were thought to be of the very highest level, comparable even to the legendary vintage of 1961, but many of the wines failed to fulfil their promise. And even the great wine critic Robert Parker was hesitant and not overly enthusiastic regarding the quality of the 1990 red Bordeaux when they were first presented.

Many of the wines that improve with ageing can taste unbalanced at an early stage because of the strength of their acidity in white wines, or their firm tannin structure in the case of red wines. However, do not fall into the trap of believing that a wine that shows well when young will not improve or that a young sharp or tough wine will automatically develop into a magic old bottle. A wine needs more than just acidity or tannin to improve.

It is slightly easier to predict that a wine might not improve than the reverse but even then you need to be cautious. I remember buying a case of Chassagne-Montrachet 1er cru Morgeot 1993 for my private cellar from Domaine Ramonet in 1995 because of the estate's very high reputation. Tasting a bottle in early 1996, I thought that the wine was rather lean and began to be anxious about its capacity for improvement; three years later I opened another bottle and discovered that I was drinking a truly exciting bottle of white Burgundy.

In my opinion assessing a wine's current quality and its future quality are two distinct exercises, even though they are interlinked. Incorporating both impressions into one overall verdict is not satisfactory. Why should we downgrade a wine if it is delicious now, just because we think it is not going to last? Unless, of course, the tasting session is purposely orientated towards the keeping quality of each wine.

Looking at photographs you have taken yourself, you can easily spot those with problems: maybe the background looks too dark or too light, or your friends are off-centre or slightly out of focus; perhaps a part of their body looks disproportionate, or their eyes look like those of vampires. If they have none of these drawbacks you can start looking for positive elements; photos in which your friends have the best expression and positioning, are in the nicest surroundings, or trigger the greatest emotions. Looking at several pictures and following that type of reasoning you could definitively say which ones are quality pictures.

You can follow the same sort of process with wine. Once you have established that there isn't anything wrong with a wine, you can start looking for its positive elements and it is from those that your quality assessment will truly begin. (Assessing quality is a different question altogether from rating wine, which will be dealt with in chapter 5.)

In my opinion five factors determine quality, and these are as follows:

NATURAL APPEARANCE
PURITY OR COMPLEXITY
DEFINITION
BALANCE
LENGTH

In addition, to assess a wine properly you need to have some basic information as to its identity, without of course knowing the name of the estate. Without this knowledge you could condemn a wine for not having enough intensity of colour when in fact it is a normal characteristic. Judging a Pinot Noir wine among a range of Merlot wines would not make sense as the wine would stand out, putting it at either a disadvantage or an advantage.

NATURAL APPEARANCE

The colour of a wine should look natural. It should not look over-extracted, which is sometimes the case with red wines because of special vinification techniques. It should not look over-clarified, as it is sometimes the

what is quality?

case with wines that have been too tightly filtered. To a certain extent a wine should look its natural age; for instance a high level of sulphur dioxide can ensure white wines keep the colour of a young wine for a very long time. Nevertheless some wines with good levels of acidity or tannin tend to mature more slowly and therefore keep a young colour rather longer without high levels of sulphur dioxide. A wine should certainly not look dull, but extreme brilliance is not always a sign of quality. In addition a wine should have the right consistency; it should not look fluid like a glass of water nor viscous like a glass of olive oil. It should look healthy and attractive.

PURITY OR COMPLEXITY

The smell of a wine should be appealing. It should exhibit either a very pure character or a multiple collection of smells.

The idea that a wine has a smell that rests mainly on one odour is often seen as a weakness and therefore such a wine cannot be considered for greatness. I disagree: a single dominant smell in a wine can have

great character if it has real purity. It is difficult to explain, but the smell should not seem synthetic or confected, it should not be overwhelming but should rather be fragrant, almost fragile, and very noticeable. It should be like a single piece of harp music played by a virtuoso with an occasional light background accompaniment from the orchestra. Of course such a smell can only come from a classic grape variety, delicately complemented by the effects of its origin. A smell of oak alone could never be described as pure.

Complexity is what most tasters are looking for in a great wine: a unique character, with not one dominant tone but several, interchanging all the time. Putting your nose in a wine like this is a privileged experience. Such complexity is normally only encountered in a wine that had enough character to begin with and has matured long enough for such a transformation to be effected. Only a few grape varieties under the right environmental conditions are capable of this.

Many tasters consider the intensity of smells to be a strong indicator of quality. I do not disagree, but I think the word intensity can be a touch misleading, since it can give the impression that the stronger the smell the better the wine, which is not the case. A wine needs to have a well-defined nose, but some can be powerful and others much lighter. It depends on the type and style of the wine: the smell must fit the style. Great Champagnes or older top-quality Pinot Noirs do not need to be powerful; often it is by their delicacy that they seduce.

DEFINITION

Wines of high quality are memorable, partly because they can almost be said to have a personality. They are more than just liquids; they produce a wonderful feel or shape in the mouth. You can talk about them, because you can almost visualise them.

Those easy-drinking wines enjoyed with many of our meals or simply quaffed in front of the TV are not to be sneered at. They fulfil a valid purpose, but most of them are forgettable because they all taste the same. Here an oaky Chardonnay tasting nicely of vanilla, there a red wine tasting vaguely of red fruit. It would be difficult to say that they have a real definition in the more holy sense of the term. They are more like an episode of a soap, enjoyable but quickly forgotten. Now compare them with the last wine that truly excited you, even if it was a while ago. No doubt it is still fresh in your mind with all the sensation, emotion and pleasure you felt when drinking it. It had definition!

BALANCE

Balance is an important concept for a wine. The main elements of a wine, its acidity, alcohol, sugar for a sweet wine or tannin for a red wine, and flavours

should all combine harmoniously. A top-quality red wine such as a great Cabernet Sauvignon will have these elements in the correct balance to make it feel powerful and rich yet not hard.

A wine can still be well balanced if one of the elements predominates as long as the others combine to counterbalance it. It is rather like scales which could be balanced with two weights on each side or with one weight against three provided that the total weight on each side was the same. The classic examples are the top sweet wines which can have a high level of residual sugar, but which, thanks to the right mix of acidity, alcohol and flavours, are still perfectly balanced and not cloying. It therefore follows that if too much of one element is not complemented by enough of the others, you are left with an unbalanced wine.

LENGTH

Length, or aftertaste, is the quality and the duration of the sensations felt just after the wine has been swallowed or spat out. For the great majority of wines that will last only a few seconds. In some cases it may be followed by a faint impression of slight acidity, dryness or even bitterness, or the opposite: a strong and inelegant aftertaste. The better wines tend to have a subtle aftertaste, leaving an appealing flavour that fades slowly. However the worth of a wine's length is not just based on its duration but also on its quality.

Furthermore, length is a factor that can easily be missed. Tasters are often still analysing the wine as it felt in the mouth, so that by the time they come to think of its aftertaste it is too late. Unless they taste the wine again they do not judge the aftertaste, which is a great shame because it is a key element of quality.

Finesse is another attribute often mentioned when considering a wine's quality, although for myself I consider it to be an amalgam of great nose, balance and length, rather than an independent aspect.

These five factors are all important and for a wine to be considered of real quality it has to fulfil the right conditions in more than just one of them. For instance a wine with a clear definition would display little quality if it did not also have purity or complexity on the nose; nor would a well-balanced wine pass the quality test if it had no real length.

For her part, Master of Wine Jane Hunt has a simple but efficient mnemonic to cover her main quality factors: BLIC which stands for: Balance, Length, Intensity, Complexity.

wine faults

When you buy a bottle of wine, you expect it to be free of any defects, but unfortunately that is not always the case. During wine-making the storage containers can taint the wine, unwanted yeast or bacteria can contaminate it, excessive or not enough contact with oxygen can lead to deterioration, additives, which are supposed to protect it, can spoil it, problems can arise during bottling (contamination or air intake), or the bottle's closure which is supposed to protect the wine can instead taint its flavour.

We are not of course talking about inferior wines that are nevertheless drinkable, but wines with an obvious defect. The principal faults are as follows:

CORK TAINT
VOLATILE ACIDITY
OXIDATION
HYDROGEN SULPHIDE
HIGH SULPHUR DIOXIDE
OTHERS

CORK TAINT

This sommelier's nightmare is by far the most common of the serious wine faults. The proportion of tainted bottles of wine can be astonishingly high; depending on the source of information, it is thought that anything from 1–8 per cent of bottles can be mildly to strongly affected. TCA (2,4,6, Trichloroanisole) is the principal compound responsible for the smell of corked wine and it is both powerful and volatile. It is thought to originate from the reaction of the phenolics in the bark of the oak tree with the chlorine used to disinfect corks (giving Trichlorophenol), and then by a further reaction with moulds developing under the moist conditions of cork storage or transport. However, other related compounds emanating from mouldy wine containers can also produce similar smells; the wooden roof of some wineries, or any wooden materials which have been treated with chlorine, can produced similar compounds that are capable of migrating into the wine because of their very volatile state. In any case, whatever its origin, the smell of wine affected by this type of compound can range from the strong smell of bark or cardboard, to a damp, musty or even mouldy cellar. The wine's natural smell is completely overpowered by that of the compound and the wine smells and tastes extremely unpleasant.

Frustratingly, this problem affects every producer who uses natural corks. So buying an expensive bottle of wine is not a guarantee of avoiding a corked wine. Nor, contrary to popular belief, are bottles of sparkling wine immune from the problem. Cork taint is not noticed so much with them, simply because most people drink sparkling wines without smelling them and they are often served so cold that the corked flavour is slightly anaesthetised.

It seems that from the late 1980s onward more bottles have been affected with cork taint. Some wine experts point the finger at the cork industry for not having introduced an efficient enough quality assurance system. However in my view one of the reasons why this problem has become more apparent is linked with two specific factors. First, consumers know, in general, far more about wine than before and therefore are more capable of spotting a faulty wine. Second, and perhaps more important, is that the average quality of wine has increased so much in the last twenty years that a faulty wine stands out much more than before.

In response to this serious problem, some wine companies have started to use alternative closures such as screw caps or plastic corks. This is an extremely efficient way of reducing cork taint (although as we have seen wine can be contaminated from other sources too). For its part, the cork industry is seriously trying to eliminate, as far as possible, the incidence of cork taint in wine. The Quercus project, an important research programme partly financed by the EU in the 1990s, was a positive initiative in that direction. New experiments in the production of cork such as the use of hydrogen peroxide rather than chlorine as a disinfectant and better application of quality assurance and control systems at all levels of production should help to achieve real progress.

VOLATILE ACIDITY (VA)

Volatile acidity results from an excessive amount of acetic acid in wine. Every wine contains some acetic acid because it is a normal by-product of fermentation, but the levels are normally low enough not to be detected by smell alone. Some sweet wines made with botrytised grapes or wines matured for a long period in wooden containers tend to have slightly higher levels than other wines, but this accords with their styles. In the EU the maximum permitted level of volatile acidity is regulated by wine type.

However with poor hygiene or high temperatures, certain strains of bacteria or occasionally yeasts can develop in the wine and cause increased production of acetic acid. A wine with a high level of acetic acid and its volatile ester, ethyl acetate, smells of nail varnish, glue or vinegar, and tastes sour, almost burning, in the mouth.

Some cheap red wines do have a definite smell of nail varnish, but buying wine from reputable wine producers should obviate the problem.

OXIDATION

Some of the components of wine may react with oxygen and transform the wine's condition for the worse. Most wines benefit from a certain amount of oxygen during wine-making, but the level and the temperature at which it happens must be controlled to avoid any deterioration. And of course many fortified wines such as tawny port, Madeira or some French vin doux naturels are matured with regular oxygen contact to impart very specific flavours.

When suffering from oxidation, both red and white wines take on a brown colour, lose their fruity aromas and taste flat in the mouth. Again, attentive wine-making ensures this problem is relatively rare in wines from reputable producers.

HYDROGEN SULPHIDE

During fermentation certain strains of yeasts can transform elemental sulphur (which originates from sulphur dusting treatments in the vineyard or from burning sulphur wicks used for cask sterilisation) into hydrogen sulphide, producing unwanted reductive odours; these can be exacerbated by specific conditions such as a lack of both nitrogen and oxygen for the yeasts to feed on. H_2S and mercaptans are the two main types of unwanted reductive odours found in wine. Wines affected by H_2S smell of rotten eggs, and can then develop mercaptans odours which make them smell of garlic or sewage but it is relatively rare to find wines affected to such an extent.

HIGH SULPHUR DIOXIDE

Sulphur dioxide (SO_2) is a preservative, used as an antioxidant and antiseptic in wine. If used too generously (maximum legal levels do exist for each wine type) the aroma of the wine can be affected by it. Wines with a high level of SO_2 give a pungent sensation on the nose with the smell of a just-struck match, and they can feel prickly in the mouth. People suffering from asthma can react badly to them.

It is quite common to find wines, especially young white wines or sweet wines, smelling strongly of SO_2.

OTHERS

Several other defects can be encountered in wine. For example a wine can have a 'geranium smell' because it has reacted to the addition of sorbic acid (for protection against yeasts). Or it can be affected by a metal or a protein haze among other faults. However, better understanding of wine-making and better quality assurance and control systems mean that these problems, unlike those above, rarely reach consumers.

LOOK-ALIKE WINE FAULTS

Tartrate crystals

In white wine these crystals look like small pieces of broken glass stuck to the underside of the cork, or at the bottom of the bottle, while in red wine they look more like tiny red diamonds. They can appear if the wine is kept at a cold temperature, and originate from the reaction, at certain temperatures, between natural components of the wine, either potassium or calcium with tartaric acid. Their presence might be an indication (but not proof) that the wine has not been submitted to cold stabilisation. If accidentally poured into a glass they normally fall to the bottom, are quite harmless and do not affect the taste of the wine.

Sediment

Sediment looks a little like black dust with a few larger particles, and is mostly encountered in quality red wines with some bottle age or in some unfiltered red wines. It results from the slow precipitation of tannin and colouring matters, which is partly why red wines lose colour and soften with ageing. Old bottles of red wine likely to have some sediment should be decanted prior to serving or at least poured very gently to avoid any sediment getting into the glass. While a little sediment will not mar the wine, a lot will make the wine murky and unpleasant to taste.

chapter 5

judging wine

Judging wine is simply putting a label on an assessment of its quality, or, in other words, giving it a sort of official stamp. It also provides a proper reference to our or someone else's judgements.

It is by no mean a new activity. Reading one of my all-time favourite wine books, *The Story of Wine* by Hugh Johnson, you will discover that at the time of the Egyptian Pharaoh Tutankhamun (who died in 1352 BC) some wines were already labelled 'very good quality'. A little more documented is the fact that under the Roman Empire the wines of Falernum (in Campania) were rated among the very best. More recently, in 1855 some brokers in Bordeaux established a classification of the best wines of the Médoc and the Graves wine areas, to be presented at the Exposition Universelle of Paris in that same year. In fact so important did this 1855 Médoc (and Graves) classification become that it is still much referred to today in fine wines departments.

Today there are few wines that escape some sort of rating, from the most prestigious ones that will answer to the palates of wine critics such as Robert Parker to much more humble ones that will submit to the verdict of journalists such as Malcolm Gluck. Most wine magazines regularly hold comparative wine tastings and publish the results with a commentary on the wines. In addition almost every wine-producing country has one or more wine competitions that will award prizes to what are thought to be the best wines. Even countries with a small or even no wine industry such as Belgium, England or Scandinavia are involved in the ratings game of judging wines from all over the planet.

wine competitions

There is no absolute definition as to what constitutes a wine competition. In the EU if certain strict but not totally comprehensive rules are observed, then official recognition will be granted for the competition. Principally, these concern the parameters of the class (the word used to designate a set of wines), the wines judged (for instance to ensure that enough samples are tasted from an area to provide a valid reference point), the judges (enough of them to be objective), and the number of awards (no more than 40 per cent of wines entered, I believe). This official validation is important in the EU as it entitles winners of the competition to advertise the fact that they have received a particular award on their wine labels. A further, but by no means compulsory, recognition can be obtained from the OIV (Office International de la Vigne et du Vin) in Paris if the competition is international and the organisers follow the OIV rules.

Comparative tastings normally run by wine magazines or newspapers are simply small versions of official competitions, and therefore most of my comments on wine competitions also apply to them.

There can be substantial variation between competitions. Factors such as the numbers of wines and their method of submission, the conditions of judging, the expertise of the tasters and what is expected of them, the marking system and the type and number of awards given can mean that competitions may have little in common. A closer look at the significance of several aspects of wine competitions can be quite revealing.

NUMBER OF WINES

The wines need to be representative of the wine style or area assessed. And to declare a wine to be a prime example in a particular area it must have been compared against a large enough number of wines to give a true picture of the style of wine in that area. There would be little value in a gold medal awarded to a Californian Chardonnay for being supposedly the best of that style in the region if it was competing against only seven other wines. There are some cases, of course, where winning an award against a small number of wines can have some value, for instance if the tasting concentrates on wines regarded as the very best of their style or area – a type of grand finale or crème de la crème – but there is still the problem of how to make the selection, by reputation or by previous competition results? In general, however, serious wine competitions do assess a considerable number of wines for each style and/or area. Indeed they are often accused of trying to judge too many wines at a time, with complaints from tasters that they are wasting too much time assessing ordinary wines. This is slightly unfair as it is not the organisers' fault if there is an abundance of wines in some categories.

Apart from the number of wines, other crucial factors will affect the competition, namely the state of the wines (finished or unfinished), their presentation, order, temperature, pedigree and finally their authenticity.

STATE OF THE WINE

Finished wines are those that have been bottled and are soon to be sold, or are already in shops so that the tasters are judging the same wines that the public can purchase. In some cases this can have a few drawbacks. For instance in a large competition, because of the amount of work involved, the results might not be published until some three to six months after the competition took place. By then some of the wines might all have been sold or even consumed, rendering the results commercially meaningless or at best simply symbolic. A more embarrassing problem could be faced by the organisers in the case of wines deteriorating during that period and therefore being past their best by the time the results are announced. Thankfully this is a rare occurrence but it can happen, particularly with some styles of fresh and fruity dry white wines that have only a very limited shelf life. The International Wine and Spirit Competition (run in Ockley, Surrey) is so aware of this problem that medal winners are chemically analysed before results are finalised and marks can be deducted for wines showing deficiencies. For example a red wine might be very smooth and pleasant to taste but if its chemical analysis shows a high pH and an extremely low level of total sulphur dioxide, there are grounds for concern as to its future.

Unfinished wines are those that are still in cask or vat and from which small samples have been drawn for the competition. These might not have been filtered and may not have completed their wine-making maturation. The problem with this style of tasting can be that the tasters are judging wines that might not exactly match those that the public will be drinking later once bottled. A wine might seem wonderful at the time of the assessment but it could lose much of its initial appeal if badly handled during its final maturation. An accusing finger is often pointed at tight filtration, especially in the case of red wines, for spoiling a potentially great wine. But it is impossible to generalise: I have tasted wines that were awarded medals when unfinished and I found them perfectly worthy of their prize long after they were bottled.

Indeed one of the most prestigious wine competitions in the world, the Jimmy Watson Trophy which takes place each year in Melbourne, is presented to the best one-year-old Australian red wine, most of the eligible wines being judged in an unfinished state. Having sampled a few of the winners I only wish that I had a few cases in my cellar.

PRESENTATION

Presentation differs between competitions too: in some the wines are presented in the glass but in others the wines are left in their bottles, which are wrapped to conceal their identities. It has been argued that seeing the shape of the bottle or even the colour of the glass at the top of the neck can influence the judgement of the tasters because they will try to guess the identity of the wine. I myself do not subscribe to this point of view. Of course cheats, trying to make a particular wine win, have more chance of succeeding if the bottles are there but unless the bottles are maladroitly wrapped or the tasters physically unwrap them there will be few clues, as similar styles of wine normally have similarly styled bottles. Besides, it is a singularly unreliable way to try to show a wine to advantage.

ORDER

The order in which the wines are presented can also have an effect on the outcome of the tasting. It is very difficult even for experienced tasters when assessing a particular wine not to be influenced by the taste of the preceding wine. For example, a slightly lighter wine might seem even lighter if following the fuller one of the set and vice versa. As reported in *La Revue du Vin de France* in October 1999, this has led to comments by some tasters that it was possible for a dishonest organiser to influence the outcome of the tasting by placing the preferred wine just after a really mediocre one to make it look even better. To be fair, in competition tasters are often free to start, within a set of wine, with any wine they like, but in general it is true that the numerical order is usually followed. Of course it is possible to present the wines to each taster in a different order. Thus Taster A could taste wine in the order 1,2,3,4; Taster B 2,4,1,3; and Taster C 3,1,4,2; but frankly it can be complicated to organise, especially if a lot of wines and tasters are involved, and can cause confusion in note-taking. Indeed one can easily imagine a taster having to record their marks in a non-consecutive order on the tasting sheet inadvertently simply writing from top to bottom and thereby putting the comments in the wrong place. If, on the other hand, each taster is given a tasting sheet according to their specific wine order then those counting the marks later will need to be extremely vigilant not to make the same sort of mistake. In most competitions the wines within each category are numbered and presented in an order based on the luck of the draw. It might not be perfect but on the whole it does work.

TEMPERATURE

Temperature, as mentioned earlier, has a real effect on our perception of the taste of a wine, so it is crucial that all wines in the same category are served at the same temperature. Nonetheless, this is rarely the case, particularly for the white wines that have to be tasted on the cool side. The difference between the first and the last wine tasted results from either the ambient temperature of the room, or, if the wines are left in an ice-bucket, the cold water altering the temperature. Even so, if the set of wines is not too big (say between ten and thirty) the change in temperature will be fairly slight and will not influence the results too much. To eliminate this problem, red or even white wines can be left in the tasting room for a few hours before the tasting to reach the ambient temperature; the disadvantage here is that tasting rooms are often on the warm side which would mean that while all the wines would be tasted at the same temperature, it could be the wrong one.

PEDIGREE

A reproach often directed at competitions is that they do not always include the very best wines. The cost of running a competition can be quite high, between organising the event (venue, equipment, tasters who are normally unpaid but whose travel expenses are reimbursed, paperwork etc.) and then marketing its results (cost of certificates, PR, perhaps a gala dinner, etc.) with the result that the wines entered in the competition are not usually bought but are donated by the producer, agent or wine merchant, although occasionally organisers buy the wines for a very specific tasting. To enter a wine in a competition, a set number of bottles have to be provided free of charge and also a fee has to be paid. Not every producer wants to incur these extra costs and, for example, an estate with a high reputation may think twice before risking it in a competition since a good result would add little to its reputation but a bad one could be very damaging. We very rarely see first-growth claret in competition. Another reason for not entering a wine in a competition may be that a small estate can sometimes sell all its wines very quickly. If as a producer you sell all your production easily why waste a few bottles and pay a fee on top? And in fact wine-makers who sell their entire production, small or not, are often also those with high reputations, giving them two reasons for not entering. It would be wrong to conclude however that wine competitions are the reserve of second-division products; big names do enter their wines in the major competitions: for instance in the

Champagne section of the London International Wine Challenge many of the top cuvées from the grandes marques are entered.

AUTHENTICITY

A real concern for both the consumer and the organiser is the genuineness of the samples being presented and tasted. Most samples originate directly from the producer or agent, and there is nothing to stop an unscrupulous competitor sending a better wine in place of an inferior one. For example a producer of a large cuvée divided into several vats could, with the competition in mind, select what they consider to be the best of them. From then on, that vat would be given special treatment, making it a far better wine than in the other vats. If the producer sends in samples from that particular vat on the understanding that it represents a blend of all the vats, they are cheating the system. Any award should apply only to the wine from that specific vat, not the entire cuvée. As in every walk of life cheats do exist but cheating in a competition is in most cases very short-sighted. In the example I gave the producer would be likely to be quickly discovered if they were to pretend that the entire batch was the same. Organisers often do retaste the wines once they are on sale, and if they receive letters of complaint or read negative comments on the standard of their winners in the press they take such opinions seriously.

In order to avoid 'la cuvée spéciale de compétition' it has been suggested that organisers could buy the wines of the estates wishing to enter the competition at random in shops and then charge the cost to the producers. In that way the wineries could not cheat. But then not every wine would have had the same storage conditions, making the validity of the competition very questionable.

TASTING CONDITIONS

Conditions for tasting can be quite different from one competition to another. An event may take place in a small room which allows only a very few tasters at the same time or it can be in a big hall where several groups of tasters judge different sets of wines. The first case can be intimidating for the tasters but the surroundings make it easy to concentrate, while the second case may put the tasters in a more relaxed mood but unfortunately with more distractions too. Tasters might be provided with tables and chairs, in very rare instances with an individual booth, or simply be left to walk between the wines carrying a clipboard. They might be given all the wines of the set to be judged at the same time or, if each taster uses the same glass throughout, they might only have one wine at a time, making comparisons more difficult. It also means that a tiny amount of the preceding wine or its smell might remain in the glass and consequently slightly modify the assessment. To be fair the glass can be washed in between wines or rinsed with a little of the new wine for tasting to avoid that problem but that is a chore and it is easy to miss a turn. I even know a place with regular serious tastings, where four or five tasters have to share the same glass of wine for each wine to be tasted. I cannot say that I am a great fan of that method. Apart from the rather unhygienic aspect, it also means that each taster will taste the wine with a different amount in the glass. The first taster of, say, wine number 7 will work from a full glass, making it difficult to swirl the wine, and also giving different information as to the depth of colour from the last taster on that glass.

Some very reputable tasters such as Steven Spurrier in *Decanter* magazine (October 1999) and Clive Coates in *Wine* magazine (January 2000) seriously question the validity of blind tasting for assessing wines. They argue that blind tasting tends to favour the same style of wine (see later in this section) and that in order to appreciate and understand totally a wine it is important to have some information about it. They have a point: certain wines can easily be misunderstood when tasted blind. A particular aspect of a wine might appear strange but once you know how it was made (from growing the grapes up to bottling) it might become clear that it is simply a normal and interesting feature of that wine. Also, knowing its pedigree and price can prevent you from being too harsh with a type of wine that from the start does not pretend to be anything but a simple quaffing wine, and the reverse applies for an expensive wine. Unfortunately however, such is human nature that in my opinion giving medals by tasting wines when you know their identity would open the door to all sorts of treachery, or at least it would bring a strong and unavoidable influence to bear on the judges. I agree that blind tasting is not perfect but it is the lesser of the two evils. I have to point out that neither Clive nor Steven is advocating knowing the wines when it comes to competition but they are drawing attention to the limits of the exercise.

Another point regarding the conditions of judging is put forward by Jacques Puisais, an eminent French oenologist, in *La Revue du Vin de France* in October 1999, who argues that because wine is often drunk with food it should not be judged only on its own but also in the context of its reaction with food. As a sommelier myself having to advise continually on matching food and wine I find the idea tempting but almost unworkable in practice. Judging a wine by its

compatibility with food would mean introducing another very subjective element into the equation, and a very variable one at that, for could the same dish be reproduced exactly each time? Food and wine is a fascinating subject but should be considered as a whole and not just as a means of assessing wine.

QUALITY OF TASTERS

Of all the contentious issues surrounding wine competitions, the most important one concerns the quality of the tasters, who are often censured for being incompetent, biased or even dishonest.

These are serious allegations as normally the tasters' backgrounds are studied carefully before they are invited to take part in serious competitions. However, just because someone works in the wine trade does not guarantee that they will make good judges, even if they are relatively good tasters themselves. In their working life they might assess wines every day with great success but they are following their own criteria. They might be selecting wine for blending, for selling in shops or for adding to a restaurant wine list. Their method of choosing will often be based on a combination of a simple tasting system and a genuine feeling for the wines, but this is very different from having to follow a precise tasting system and rate each wine very accurately. I remember when Robert Joseph first invited me to judge at the Wine Challenge in the early 1990s. It was the first time I was going to be a judge in an official competition and on the one hand I felt very proud, but on the other I was worried because I did not want my marking to be too out of line with the other tasters.

As a result of these concerns, more and more competitions have started to run an 'open day' for their tasters, especially new ones, giving them instruction and advice on how to mark the wines. Some competitions also set tasters a test, of which they may or may not be aware, prior to inviting them to be a judge. During the open day the beginners are given sets of wines to mark but some might be slightly doctored or be duplicated, in order to see if the judges can spot a wine with a high level of volatile acidity, or mark two identical glasses of wine in the same manner. These types of exercises are extremely helpful and all tasters should regularly submit themselves to them as a way of training their senses and knowing their strong and weak points. Judging a person on one performance alone can of course be deceptive: we all have good and bad days. As I am writing this book, Manchester United, after twenty-five games, is top of the Premier League, but last Sunday they lost 3–0 to Newcastle, only their third defeat of the year so far. If independent critics after seeing that game were to say that Man Utd are really a poor team and should sack their manager, they would be laughed down. Similarly even good

tasters have their ups and downs. Personal factors (such as tiredness, mood) or external ones (such as the order of the wines, a new marking system) can easily alter our perception. In Australia, before becoming a fully sanctioned judge for the big states wine competitions, you have to serve as an apprentice for a certain length of time. The seriousness and consistency of Australian wine competition judging speak for themselves.

Another possibility is that some experienced tasters are assigned to the wrong type of wines. In large competitions wines as varied as light dry white wines, dark and rich fortified wines or pink sparkling wines can be included, and even in small local competitions involving wines of a similar style, judges from other areas are occasionally invited. So it is not impossible to imagine that a Champagne wine-maker could be confronted with a set of fortified wines from the south of France; unless they are real aficionados of fortified wines, their judgement could be less than reliable. Usually competition organisers check the area of expertise of each taster but mistakes can occur or the organisers can simply be given the wrong information. Or sometimes the organisers might deliberately seek to include people from other specialities to bring in new ideas and opinions. And why not? After all, having wines judged from a different angle might add a refreshing side to the competition. Nevertheless, very specific wines should be left to the experts; for instance if you are not used to tasting cask samples your marking will be extremely unreliable.

Even within an area of expertise, the origin of the tasters in the trade plays a part in the judging. Growers, oenologists, producers, wine buyers, shop managers, brokers, journalists and sommeliers do not assess wine in the same manner or with the same philosophy. It is very unlikely, for instance, that a set of Bordeaux wines would get the same ranking from a jury composed of oenologists and one composed of journalists or sommeliers, even if they all worked in Bordeaux. That is not really surprising since each sector has different priorities. Oenologists are said to be mainly concerned with faultless wines, whereas journalists or sommeliers are more interested in finding original, expressive wines. That is something of a caricature but none the less contains a kernel of truth and has led to demands for tasting panels to include people from different areas of the wine trade.

Opinion on the same wines can also vary greatly among people from different areas or countries: culture, tradition and habits quite naturally influence our taste. The British wine magazine *Decanter* came up with the idea for their April 1999 issue of arranging for the same set of wines – ten Chardonnays, principally from California – to be tasted at the same time by a panel in London and one in New York. Interestingly, the Chardonnay that came out top in London could

only manage ninth place in New York, while the number one in New York finished in seventh place in London! While it doesn't prove the point, it certainly hints at its possibility.

One viewpoint sometimes expressed is that the majority of tasters tend to favour the same styles of wine over any other. So it is said that a wine is more alluring and has a better chance of winning if it has a beautiful colour; an intense character on the nose, either oaky or varietal; an alcohol level on the high side; and acidity or tannins that are not overpowering. In other words tasters are accused of rewarding what the French call 'les bêtes de concours' (show animals) and ignoring the more subtle wines. Some wines inevitably get overlooked in competition; as Robert Joseph put it in *Wine & Spirit International* in August 1999: 'After all, there are some very good actors who will never win Oscars! Anyone who is involved with wine competitions and does not acknowledge that is being dishonest. It is a fact that some great white Burgundies, to take but one example, will never win a gold medal in competitions because of their style which makes them very difficult to taste blind.' Undeniably wines with an idiosyncratic character are at a disadvantage because they are more difficult to understand. However, while it may be true that a certain level of injustice occurs, there is also a large measure of sour grapes from some losers. Tasters in

general come from a cross-section of the wine industry and as such provide a broad spectrum of current opinion. They cannot be wrong all the time.

Inevitably in a discipline which involves so many people and where subjectivity plays such a large part the idea is occasionally mooted that some treachery might be afoot. This suggestion is largely due to the fact that tasters taking part in a competition sometimes have a vested interest in the wines they are tasting. Organisers naturally invite people familiar with the style of wine to be tasted and occasionally it might happen that one or more of their own wines will be included in the selection. However, because the wines are almost always tasted blind, it is far from certain that the tasters will automatically recognise their own wine among others of a similar character. Furthermore, they might not in fact know that one of their wines is in the tasting because tasters are not normally told the names of the estates beforehand. In any case, organisers are not fools and will be extremely vigilant of the marking in those cases. Often, too, tasters representing a wine included in the tasting are told that their mark for that wine will not be taken into consideration.

MARKING

Depending on the competition the tasters may be expected to assess wines in different ways. They may be asked to taste unfinished or finished wines. They may be expected to assess a small number of wines (up to twenty) or a very large number (more than a hundred) in one session. Some styles are easier to taste than others; for instance it is always difficult to taste a large number of young and very tannic red wines. Tasters may be permitted to mark the wines as they choose or, on the contrary, may have to favour certain characteristics. In some official regional competitions, for example, tasters are encouraged to mark down wines that are not typical of the area, even if they are good wines. They may have to follow a very rigid tasting and scoring system or simply come up with a mark for each wine. Some competitions provide tasters with a sophisticated tasting grid that is so complicated that it can alter their assessment. All such information about the type of tastings should be given to anyone invited to attend so that they can decline the invitation if they do not agree with the system to be used. Tasting and marking should be done in complete silence without conferring with the other tasters or trying to influence them.

The system of marking varies from competition to competition. Some use the 100 system, others mark out of 20 points, others out of 7 or 5; the possibilities are endless. However, rather than the overall number of points, it is the way the final mark for each wine is arrived at that is the sensitive issue. The method most often used is to calculate an average mark for every wine by adding up the score for each and dividing it by the number of tasters. A slight variation is to eliminate the best and the worst mark for each wine and then calculate its average. Both systems work well but they are criticised for resulting in a compromise rather than truly reflecting the individual marks given to the wines. Indeed as the New York wine importer and wholesaler Barry Bassin points out in *Decanter*: 'A typical scenario has a panel of six voting a given wine, say, three recommendations for gold and three for bronze. The result: silver. Note, please, that no one actually voted silver.' Other rating methods do exist. For example the US magazine *Tastings: The Journal of the Beverage Testing Institute* uses a system based on the mode method, where the score that occurs most frequently determines how the wines are rated. For anyone interested in the pros and cons of all the various statistical methods, I suggest reading *Wines: Their Sensory Evaluation* by Maynard A. Amerine and Edward B. Roessler. Suffice it to say that as soon as several people are involved there will be diverse opinions, and the result, whatever the method, can only be a compromise (although maybe a happy one).

AWARDS

The final sensitive issues concerning wine competitions are the type and above all the number of awards given to the wines. Most competitions are based on the system of the Olympic Games. Gold, silver and bronze medals are the most common type of award, although unlike at the Olympics more than one gold, silver and bronze is often presented in each section. This means that it is not only the finest wine that gets the gold but also every wine that reaches a given standard. In many cases there are also trophies for wines considered to be the best in their category. So there may be none, one or more gold medals in a category plus a trophy above them. Similarly below bronze certain competitions award a type of commendation referred to humorously by the French as a chocolate medal. Some competitions present a top award for the most outstanding wine overall as does the UK Vineyards Association with its Gore-Brown Trophy. The International Wine Challenge has recently created two new trophies: one to reward innovation (the James Rogers Trophy); and the other to reward consistency over five years of competing (the Len Evans Trophy).

The large number of awards in each competition is a source of some concern. According to *La Revue du Vin de France* in October 1999 the average number of awards given represents around 28–30 per cent of the entrants and that does not even include the lower commendations. This may seem a high proportion but it might simply reflect the much improved quality of the wines. Or it may be that producers who know that their wines do not stand a chance do not bother to enter them. Wishful thinking? A more cynical explanation could be that organisers want to see wines returning to the competition the following year, so they cannot afford to be too elitist.

Certainly the quantity of awards can be confusing for consumers. It is easy to assume that the award is given to the estate whereas in most cases it is for a specific wine. A gold medal 1997 Chardonnay might not even get a bronze medal for its 1998 version, although some consumers will buy the 1998 wine based on the previous year's award.

THE POINT OF COMPETITIONS

So not everything is perfect in the world of wine competitions and tastings. But does it matter? After all, it is not as if there is only one wine competition in the world that pretends to have all the answers. On the whole I think competitions reward good wines. It seems to me that competition is good for the wine trade and by setting standards they help to improve the quality of wine. Competitions help to promote the industry and provide information and guidance to consumers and professionals alike. They inspire and motivate producers all over the world by allowing comparisons; they encourage experimentation and reveal new styles and new estates. No doubt wine monuments such as Grange, Mas la Plana, Sassicaia or Cloudy Bay would have been discovered without competitions or comparative tastings but by winning prizes they were brought to our attention earlier than might otherwise have been the case. Some tastings have even become landmarks in wine history. When Steven Spurrier was preparing his 1976 Paris tasting to compare some top red Bordeaux estates against some top Californian Cabernet Sauvignons, and some top white Burgundies against some top Californian Chardonnays he probably never dreamed of the sensation it would cause and that more than twenty years later people would still talk about it. In both the white and red sections the winner was Californian, chosen by some of the most reputable French tasters of the time! What a coup! *Longue vie aux concours!*

Robert Parker and the 100 points system

The saying goes roughly like this: 'If he gives a wine less than 90 points no one wants to buy it, but if he gives it more than 90 points no one can afford it!' Any wine enthusiast will have guessed that the person credited with such power is of course Robert Parker and the saying is what Tim Atkin refers to as the Parker Paradox. The famous wine critic is not the first person to award marks to wine, but no one before him had managed to attract such attention. Wine merchants, brokers, auctioneers and even, on occasion, restaurateurs, do not hesitate to quote his markings, especially if the scores are favourable. His ratings are very influential in the fine wine market.

Robert Parker is an American who fell in love with wine in his twenties and, unhappy with how wine was reported in the USA, he started to publish his own newsletter on wine in 1978. His strong backing for the 1982 red Bordeaux at an early stage while other critics hesitated, seems to have played an important part in his subsequent reputation. Since then he has written several books on wine and become even more influential. But increasing fame has brought criticism too. Complaints focus on the fact that his judgement, no matter how good, is only that of one man, and that his 100 points system is misleading.

He is often accused of favouring rich, concentrated wines with a pronounced oaky flavour and overlooking wines with a more delicate complexion. Parker refutes this allegation by referring to his newsletter and books where numerous, delicate wines score very high marks and concludes that his detractors do not read his publications very carefully, if at all.

However once you understand his personal taste and his rating system you are guaranteed consistency of assessment. As we saw earlier, one problem with panel judging is a lack of consistency where one panel might rate a wine great, while another finds it simply good. Since 1996 Robert Parker has taken on an assistant, Pierre-Antoine Rovani, but they have divided the wine areas of the world between them and it is quite clear who has tasted what. It takes a lot of courage to rate wines on your own; there is no hiding behind other judges. I sometimes see tasters who do not even want to take a position in front of just a handful of colleagues, but the least that one can say about Parker is that he can scarcely be accused of sitting on the fence. His assessment will be scrutinised by the world of wine experts, so he cannot afford to be complacent. This of course applies to any famous critics, such as Stephen Tanzer or Clive Coates, who publish their marking in an equally detailed fashion.

Can Robert Parker be right all the time? Of course not! But nor does he claim to be; he simply puts forward his opinion. Nevertheless it is difficult not to be impressed by the seriousness of his work and the amount of detailed information he gives his readers. There is no denying that he works hard and with a real passion. His crusade for unfiltered wines is a perfect illustration of his concern for and commitment to quality. I doubt if there are many serious wine professionals, even those who do not especially agree with his opinions, who have not on occasion used or even relied on some of his work.

It is not his fault if his markings are religiously used in the fine wine market thanks to his promotion of his 100 points system. However it would be really unfair not to give some credit to the quality of his judgement, even though like everyone he is not infallible.

Nor is Robert Parker the only pundit to enjoy a cult following. In the UK Malcolm Gluck has a similar power at the less expensive end of the wine market. Retail outlets offer such a plethora of wines that it is scarcely surprising that consumers so often turn to experts for advice.

Wines had been rated before Robert Parker but rarely on a scale of 100. And if, before Parker, tasters used a numeric system, of 1–10 or up to 20, they would usually convert their findings into compact descriptions such as mediocre or outstanding, or else use a classic 1–5 star system. So before Robert Parker came on the scene consumers were never given a wine rating that expressed such accuracy; for instance in the fifth edition of his *Wine Buyer's Guide* Parker gives 91 to Le Pin 1996 and 93+ to Le Pin 1995.

The Parker system works roughly like this: a wine is given 50 points to start, then up to 5 points are awarded for its appearance, up to 15 points for its nose, up to 20 points for its palate and aftertaste and up to 10 points for its overall impression and ageing potential. Which produces ratings something like this: outstanding wines between 90 and 100; good to very good between 80 and 89; pleasant and straightforward between 70 and 79; while below 70 most wines are considered to be of mediocre quality. Other publications (*US Wine Spectator* for instance) also use a 100 points system and while they might have slightly different ways of reaching their numbers, basically the principles are similar.

The main criticisms directed at the 100 points system are that it gives an overly scientific impression, does not describe the taste of the wine, and limits the choice of wines.

When two wines of similar style are rated at 87 and 88 one might easily believe that some scientific method was used, so authoritative and definite does it sound. Unfortunately the human palate is not capable of such exactitude. Judges rarely agree on a wine and even the same person will seldom rate the same wine consistently, although if they follow their own regular marking system the marks should be very close.

So perhaps if consistent accuracy with numbers is impossible it would be more honest to use descriptions such as excellent, good or poor. But the problem is that words can be interpreted in different ways. The word genius was once attributed to people such as Mozart or Einstein, it is now quite commonly used to describe a

footballer or tennis player. What would a rating from Parker of 'excellent' tell us about a wine? One of the very best he has tasted; a wine he thought was quite pleasant; or simply a nice little wine, especially if you consider the price? It would be hard to say. However, when he rates a wine 87, we know he thinks it is better than the wine he rated 85 and in addition we can measure how far that wine is from being among the very best he has tasted. It might not be scientifically accurate but at least it is informative.

Robert Parker does not pretend to be some sort of superhero. In a long interview given to *Decanter* magazine in June 1999 he answers John Stimpfig on the scientific accuracy of his marking by saying that he never proclaimed that it as such, but instead that his marking is simply an individual point of view. In addition he rightly talks of the double standards of some of his critics who use a 20 points system with half marks, making in effect a 40 points system very close to his 100, which is really a 50 points system as each wine starts with 50 points!

It is not Parker who has created this feeling of absolute truth. It is those in the trade who are happy to use his work and simply parrot his scoring on their lists. But who can blame them? There aren't many wine professionals who have the opportunity to taste even a fraction of the wine he does. After all, brokers, wine merchants, shop managers or sommeliers will taste new wines regularly at trade tastings or on visits to wineries, but they also have their work to do, while Robert Parker rates wine as a full-time job. So in our frantic societies where speed is king, he is a wonderful source of information and, I dare say, a fairly reliable judge.

Numbers do not describe the taste of wine. Of course they don't, any more than when a writer tells us that this wine is fine, elegant or ordinary. Naturally wine descriptions are very important in order to understand a particular wine, but just as disagreements are commonplace regarding wine rating, consensus on the description of any wine is no simple affair. Apart from very aromatic grapes such as Muscat or Sauvignon Blanc which often manage to reconcile tasters, there are many occasions when describing the smells of a wine that somebody's liquorice will be somebody's else's tobacco. Similar disagreements, albeit less marked, occur when describing the appearance or the texture of a wine. So to argue that descriptions are far more useful for the consumer than a quality rating is debatable. This depends very much on the quality of the describer. But at the risk of seeming completely 'Parkerised' myself (dear Robert, I hope you will not forget to send me – free of charge *bien sûr*! – your next book) for people relying on wine descriptions his books are not lacking. It is simply much easier to use his scoring because as Larry Walker remarks in *Wine and Spirit International* in September 1994: 'All wine judgement is subjective, whether by word or number, but because numbers appear to be scientific, they carry more weight than words.' However, so as not to be misleading, I ought to point out that Larry's article was not in favour of number rating!

Both Gerald Asher, a journalist from *Gourmet* magazine, and Master of Wine Anthony Hanson are of the opinion that the 100 points system restricts our choice of wines (*Decanter*, September 1998). They believe that more and more wines, especially red wines, are produced to a formula in order to secure a high rating. These are described as the TEC wines, standing for the wine-making principles of Technology, Extraction and Colour, including of course maximum barrel ageing to impress the consumer. Gerald remarks that some wonderful Bordeaux wines do not even find their way into the USA because buying decisions are based on the 100 points systems used by many publications. As a result, most Bordeaux wines now available in the USA are not shaped, as in the past, by the vineyard and the vintage, but by techniques calculated to achieve a high rating.

There is certainly some truth in what they say, as shown by the emergence of some new small estates humorously called 'Les Garagistes'. Many of their wines have a very deep colour, are extremely intense and quite oaky on the nose and are lusciously rich in the mouth. I have to confess that on occasion I like to drink some of these wines. The importance of the 100 points system has undoubtedly accelerated the speed of these estates' newly acquired fame. But trends have existed in wine in the past and will no doubt recur in the future, any excesses usually being corrected with time. And there are sufficient numbers of wine critics crusading for the importance of finesse and elegance that there is little risk of having only blockbuster wines available. So in fairness, while the 100 points system may have lessened our choice of wines in the top category, it has also contributed to the elimination of many substandard wines. Indeed nobody can deny that because of this particular trend for rich, smooth and full-flavoured wines, in particular red ones, many wine-makers are now reducing their yields and taking more risks by harvesting later to produce fruitier and riper wines.

For myself I have to admit that I do refer to Parker's scoring. For instance, if I wanted to buy a small quantity of wine, such as one case of an older vintage of a top-growth Bordeaux, the merchant is not going to open a bottle for me to taste. In this instance both Robert Parker and his 100 points system are useful tools in supplying information that will help me come to a decision. Robert Parker and his ratings are not there to be followed religiously but rather to be consulted and on occasion challenged in good spirit.

Whatever we think of wine rating, we all assess wine in our own way. It might not be on a points scale but at the very least it could be liking, disliking or being unsure about the taste of a wine. However, how many people would stop there? If presented with three wines they like, most people would probably find one they love (one with a spicy flavour maybe), one they really like and one they just like. They would instinctively have made a ranking assessment from their own perception of the quality of the wines.

So if we are naturally inclined to prefer one and rank others among many then a system might prove useful. It would help us to be more accurate and hence more consistent, as well as helping us to gain a better appreciation of wine, thereby increasing our confidence. While no system will produce consistently infallible results, I believe that a system can be a useful tool for assessing quality and translating it into a meaningful figure. In the same way, a political opinion poll cannot be accurate to the exact percentage, other than by sheer luck, but if the survey has been carried out conscientously, it should prove fairly correct in its predictions.

Knowing what to look for and how to interpret your findings are key, so it is vital that the method you choose really suits you. You might like to use 100 points, 20 points, three medals or any other system you prefer. Steven Spurrier in the March 1998 issue of *Decanter* explained that he had switched from the 20 points system to the five stars system because the quality of the wines produced was generally of such a good standard that five marks were enough to get the message across. The measurement you use is not so important; what is, of course, is how you reach your final figure. After all if you saw a wine rated as gold in one magazine, 9/10 in another or 96/100 by Robert Parker, each rating would lead you to expect this wine to be very good.

I use a 20 points rating system because this is the one I feel most comfortable with and find easiest to use. However, the detail of the 100 points system can be very helpful for consumers and I sometimes convert my results into a figure based on 100 points.

I have long been fascinated by the numerous rating systems created by professional tasters and wine schools around the world. Even though the aim is generally fairly similar, the manner of achieving it can be completely different, because they are used by different sections of the wine trade for slightly varied purposes.

my system

For instance, an assessment method designed by oenologists might put stronger emphasis on structural aspects of the wine, whereas another might be more concerned with rewarding certain aromatic elements.

My main criticisms of most tasting systems is that they are either too vague and consequently leave too much liberty to the tasters, or that they are so complicated that their use becomes counter-productive. If a system leaves too much to interpretation, it becomes unreliable, worth little more than assessment by gut reaction. For instance, in some methods under the appraisal of the aromas of the wine, tasters are given room to record its intensity, its character and then to rate it from faulty up to truly excellent, which will be given a mark. In my opinion the system should help the taster to interpret the signals more clearly. For example, more specific comments will be prompted by asking: Why did you not rate the smell of this wine as excellent? Was it not pure enough or was it too obviously oaky?

Conversely, having too many instructions can lead to some strange results. It is rather like drawing a landscape: unless you constantly keep an eye on the overall picture you could end up with some elements out of proportion. Too many subdivisions can cancel each other out or dilute the weight of some important factors. Furthermore, looking at a wine in so much detail is tiring and you can easily lose concentration.

I have seen a tasting card for red wine where in the third section (the palate) of the analysis alone there were sixteen subdivisions among which were taste satisfaction, cleanliness of flavour, pleasantness of flavour, complexity of flavour, intensity of flavour, vinosity, overall impression of taste and flavour, all worth 3 points each. When all the subdivisions of the three sections were added up a maximum score of 100 points was possible. This card was drawn up by a wine expert who has written a book on tasting full of good and sensible advice, but while it might work for him, I found the system simply too cumbersome.

In comparison, another scoring card for a wine competition in another country offers only six subdivisions under the palate section: soundness, intensity, body, harmony, aftertaste and harmony (I assume this second harmony is for the aftertaste) all of which carry 8 marks, so that all the three sections come to a possible total of 100 points.

For me a good practical system must be precise and methodical, but easy to use. It must assess the important elements of the wine while keeping in mind its overall impression. The following system is one that I have designed from a combination of my experience of many wine-tasting books and tasting cards. I do not pretend that it is the perfect method but it suits my personality very well.

It is classically divided into appearance, nose and palate. The appearance is judged as a whole, as is the nose, but the palate is divided into four sections with a possible overall total of 20 points. How to use it will be explained later on in the chapter.

Scoring

Appearance	maximum = **3** points	minimum = **1.5** points
Nose	maximum = **5** points	minimum = **2.5** points
Palate	maximum = **12** points	minimum = **6** points
Structure	*maximum = 3 points*	*minimum = 1.5 points*
Flavour	*maximum = 3 points*	*minimum = 1.5 points*
Balance	*maximum = 3 points*	*minimum = 1.5 points*
Length	*maximum = 3 points*	*minimum = 1.5 points*
Total	maximum = **20** points	minimum = **10** points

Each category is broken down into half marks as follows:

	Faulty	*Inferior*	*Average*	*Superior*	*Exceptional*
Appearance	0	1.5	2	2.5	3
Nose	0	2.5	3 (3.5)	4 (4.5)	5
Structure	0	1.5	2	2.5	3
Flavour	0	1.5	2	2.5	3
Balance	0	1.5	2	2.5	3
Length	0	1.5	2	2.5	3
Total	Just one 0 and the wine is eliminated	**10**	**13/(13.5)**	**16.5/(17)**	**20**

By using half marks, even though the minimum mark is 10 points and the maximum 20, my system allows for 21 possible final scores.

Full rating scale and its interpretation:

POINTS	
10/10.5/11	**Mediocre**
11.5/12/12.5	**Ordinary**
13/13.5/14	**Average**
14.5/15/15.5	**Above average**
16/16.5/17	**Splendid** (Bronze)
17.5/18/18.5	**Magnificent** (Silver)
19/19.5/20	**Exceptional** (Gold)

In my system a wine cannot get less than 10 points, not because it starts its rating with 10 points but because if in one of the six sections it only scores 0 it is automatically eliminated. I do not rate any wine under 10 points because I consider that if a serious defect is noticeable in any one section, the wine is not fit for drinking and therefore not marketable. Indeed what would be the point of a wine having a final score of 8 points because it is slightly corked? I use cork taint as an example but if the wine was murky or extremely acidic as to be undrinkable that would be exactly the same. There is no need to give a final score to a faulty wine just because it seemed acceptable in another section: it must at least be sound overall.

HOW IT WORKS

Each mark in each section must be allocated according to some clear guidelines, which will point the tasters towards the most important considerations.

appearance (on 3 points)

0 Points = Faulty

The wine is eliminated. It might be murky or cloudy or showing a slight veil because it is affected by some wine sickness. Thanks to technology and quality assurance systems this is extremely rare nowadays. A wine might show some tartrate crystal or sediment but these are not faults (see faults section in chapter 4 pages 96–9).

1.5 Points = Inferior

The appearance is not faulty but it shows one of the following:

Colourless (for white)

Very light for its style (for red)

Overly matured (for its age)

Too extracted, looks too heavy for its style

Too much CO_2 (for still wine)

Confected, too shiny and slightly artificial colour

2 Points = Average

The wine looks normal, nothing to be excited about, but no worrying aspects either.

2.5 Points = Superior

The appearance of the wine is balanced (brilliance, colour, intensity), and inspires confidence. Most wines should fall into this category.

3 Points = Exceptional

The appearance is very attractive; either still immature so a long way to go, or some truly wonderful colour in relation to the wine style.

nose

The smell of the wine is of the utmost importance, and under my system, this is the section with the greatest value. In many systems, points are given not only for the attractiveness of the aromas, but also for their strength. Although not completely misleading, I feel that some very good wines underscore because they lack a bit of intensity on the nose. So, in this section, each mark matches two different types of wines: the more extrovert wines (A); and the more reserved ones (B). The best wines are those that achieve harmony between the quality and strength of their aromas. In the extrovert category we are more likely to find young wines made from aromatic grapes or by wine-making methods that tend to emphasise smells. In the reserved we will find older wines or those made with less stress on the strength or the smells.

0 Points = Faulty

The wine is either corked or has too much volatile acidity or some other classic fault (see wine faults section in chapter 4 pages 96-9) and is consequently eliminated.

2.5 Points = Inferior

A) Artificial (synthetic): the wine is not faulty, but it is inelegant and has a slightly chemical (confected) smell or smells strongly and coarsely rustic.

B) Bland: again no real fault, but the nose is weak and the only smells are not very inspiring, almost stale.

3 Points = Average

A) Obvious: perfectly acceptable but strong with no finesse. For instance smelling exclusively of oak.

B) Simple: very little character but not unpleasant.

3.5 Points = Above average

A) Assertive: a bit more definition, but still very powerful with not a great deal of character.

B) Straightforward: a touch of character but not enough to be very exciting.

4 Points = Superior

A) Exuberant (fruit-driven): the character is there and well defined, powerful and attractive, but it is very one-dimensional.

B) Restraint: the character is more present and shows potential, but could be a touch more pronounced.

4.5 Points = Magnificent

A) Perfumed: the character is well defined but not too exuberant, thus making it more subtle and more elegant.

B) Fragrant: the delicate character starts to show some beautiful variation, a truly wonderful nose.

It is at this point and at this point only that the two styles of nose almost meet. Extrovert ones have toned down a bit, but not yet completely, to be uniquely pure; on the other hand the reserved ones have really started to express a multitude of odours although they are not quite yet so fabulously complex.

5 Points = Exceptional

A) Purity: the nose is extremely pure, dominated, but not overpowered, by one beautiful smell. In addition it is enhanced by a few additional and lighter aromas. It is as if the wine had toned down the intensity of its perfume to gain a better balance.

B) Complex: the nose is sensational, but it is almost impossible to describe and name the smells, for the nose is constantly changing and surprising us by its unique character.

palate: structure

Structure is the shape of the wine in your mouth. Does it feel full-bodied and round, or fresh and crisp? It is important to look for its definition.

0 Points = Faulty

The wine has a serious problem: it may be terribly tough, sharp or oily (a very rare wine fault).

1.5 Points = Inferior

The wine is shapeless or deformed: it either lacks acidity and feels flat, or else has too much and feels sharp. It can feel heavy due to too much alcohol.

2 Points = Average

The wine is pleasant but it lacks definition and its shape, body and texture are difficult to categorise. It is simply not memorable by its mouthfeel.

2.5 Points = Superior

The wine is well defined, it shows its shape and body but it just misses having a truly superb texture.

3 Points = Exceptional

The wine has a perfectly defined structure with a great texture: round and velvety, supple and silky, juicy and very fresh, firm but very ripe. In other words the wine is well designed and has a great feel.

palate: flavour

As explained by Jancis Robinson in *The Oxford Companion to Wine*, the word flavour can be used either for the overall impression felt on the nose and the palate (aroma, acidity, sweetness, bitterness, astringency, etc.) or simply for the smell of the wine. I use it in this latter sense to denote the smell of the wine felt in the palate only, as I use aroma, smell or bouquet for the nose.

0 Points = Faulty

Wrong type of flavour, corked, hydrogen sulphide, etc. (see wine faults section in chapter 4 pages 96–9).

1.5 Points = Inferior

Not very elegant flavour, drinkable but unenjoyable.

2 Points = Average

The wine has a simple flavour, not unforgettable but perfectly adequate.

2.5 Points = Superior

The flavour is appealing, but lacks sufficient dimension to be truly thrilling.

3 Points = Exceptional

The palate is full of wonderful flavours of real distinction.

palate: balance

Balance is a crucial factor in the quality of wine. It is based on a combination of structure and flavour and how they fit together: a wine might have too full a flavour for a light structure, or the reverse.

0 Points = Faulty

Completely unbalanced, aggressive, something has gone wrong, perhaps too much volatile acidity or sulphur dioxide.

1.5 Points = Inferior

Just drinkable but not very enjoyable: either sharp, tough, too sweet, burning (too alcoholic), hollow, or over extracted. Best used in sangria or mulled wine.

2 Points = Average

The wine is not unpleasant, but it has definitely one component out of sync with the others.

2.5 Points = Superior

The wine is balanced and pleasant, but it could have a bit more flavour in relation to its body, etc.

3 Points = Exceptional

The wine has everything in order, and the structure and flavour work perfectly together.

palate: length

0 Points = Faulty

Terrible aftertaste: the sensation left in the mouth is extremely bitter or overly acidic; wine is undrinkable.

1.5 Points = Inferior

A touch of bitterness or sourness dominates, but fortunately that does not last long enough to make the wine undrinkable. Another possibility is that the wine has a strong aftertaste but it is not very elegant, almost cloying, such as a heavy and ordinary oak flavour.

2 Points = Average

The wine is fine, but has a fairly indifferent finish, nothing wrong but not enough flavour. Quite a lot of wines will fall into this category.

2.5 Points = Superior

The wine finishes on a really nice positive note, but it does not last very long.

3 Points = Exceptional

The aftertaste has all the right ingredients, it has an attractive flavour and definitely lasts after swallowing or spitting.

My system does not include a section for an overall impression of the wine. Many scoring systems based on 20 points might leave 3 points for the overall impression, while those based on 100 points might leave 10 or more. I find it hard to see the purpose of that final marking. If the main aspects of the wine, and in particular its balance, have been judged correctly, there is no need for an overall view since this will only confirm the assessment already made. Can you imagine a wine getting a cumulated mark of 17 points out of 17, prior to the final overall assessment and then being given only 1 point in that section, and another wine getting 8 points out of 17 and then being given 2 points for this final part? If it is purely there to record the feeling the taster has for the wine, then a strong element of hedonism is integrated in the system. There is nothing wrong with that but in such a case the taster is not only judging quality, but also measuring their own individual pleasure.

My method, apart from the nose section, works very much by deciding whether in each section the wine is awful, poor, okay, good or superb. I find it differentiates sufficiently without over-complicating or allowing too many scores in each section.

chapter 6

tasting notes

To the outsider, these strange scribbles, so-called tasting notes, must look more like the secret formulae of an alchemist than the exact impressions of a sane person! Nevertheless, they fulfil important functions in wine-tasting. They allow us to record and capture a feeling. The taste of the wine that you are drinking might seem quite obvious now but how will you remember it in two days, two weeks, two months, or even two hours? If it is a wine you found superb and that you enjoyed on a very special occasion such as your birthday, there is a good chance that the taste will linger in your memory for a long time, but there are many instances when you might only remember that the wine was red. Unless, of course, you took the time to jot down a few meaningful words. Quite apart from the actual taste of the wine, well-recorded tasting notes are capable of triggering reminiscences of the entire occasion, the place, the time and the people, bringing back all sorts of fond memories.

For wine professionals recording is essential. On many occasions we are confronted with a very large array of wines to taste in a very short space of time. After a long tasting session it would be easy to get confused and not remember exactly which wines we had been impressed with. For example, sitting on the train returning from a wine exhibition, how would we remember from among the fifty or so different Mosel Rieslings we tasted which three or four were so outstanding and why, if it wasn't for the tasting notes we recorded on the spot and through which we can now browse at leisure?

Buying decisions are often made long after the tasting sessions. Indeed most buyers want time to think and weigh up the worth of the wines they have tasted, rather than being faced with a salesperson who wants a quick decision. In contrast, tasting notes should be recorded straight away, while tasting; waiting even just a few minutes after the glass has disappeared can make them imprecise and therefore unreliable.

Wine-makers rely a great deal on the notes they write during their monitoring of unfinished wines. When blending several vats the decision as to which will go into the top cuvée and which into the second is often determined by the tasting notes of each vat. Tasting notes are indispensable tools of their profession.

The logical step on from recording information about a wine is to pass it on. Tasting notes enable us to communicate the character and quality of a wine which cannot be done just by giving its price or its identity. This communication can be verbal, from salespeople in wine shops or from sommeliers in restaurants, or in print from wine merchants' lists or by journalists' articles. Which wine lover hasn't been tempted to buy a particular bottle of wine after reading or hearing an enthusiastic description of it by someone whose opinion you trust?

Another aspect of writing tasting notes, often underestimated, is that it is an excellent method of developing our tasting skills, forcing tasters to focus completely on the wines they are assessing. Writing a well-thought-out description is the best way to improve someone's perception and understanding of any wine. It does sometimes feel like a chore, especially when there is a large number of wines, but, believe me, if you persevere you will be well rewarded.

It is important here to mention that wine rating, as seen in the previous chapter, cannot be considered to be a tasting note. Simply giving a mark to a wine does not describe its flavour or its mouthfeel. However, a mark can be part of a tasting note and in effect can form its conclusion.

While it is not difficult to appreciate the role of tasting notes, their exact worth can be rather more ambiguous. Can we really gain a feel for a wine just by reading its tasting notes? If I had to give just a quick answer, I would compare a tasting note to a photofit, similar to those seen in newspapers or on the television, where a likeness of a crime suspect has been produced by police from eye-witness descriptions. It's the same for a wine: tasting notes can never replicate the real sensation but they can often give a good idea of a wine's character and quality.

The extent to which the attributes of the wine are successfully conveyed depends partly on the skills of the writer and partly on the level of wine appreciation possessed by the reader. I am not saying that only people in the know can understand tasting notes, but this is more likely to be the case. Often derided by outsiders, tasting notes are sometimes even compared to an exclusive language that only initiates can comprehend. However, this is not strictly true, as the vocabulary is mostly from everyday speech. Telling people who know little about wine that a wine is very perfumed and dry, even if it does not convey an exact description, should at least give them some indication as to the taste of the wine.

The two key aspects of tasting notes are their length and content, both of which are greatly influenced by several different but interrelated factors: the time allocated for the tasting, the occasion and the place, the quality of the wines, the skills and experience of the tasters, and, for those in the wine trade, their jobs and aims.

The length of tasting notes is largely dictated by circumstance. Clearly, if you are short of time at a large tasting you would write less than if you had all the time in the world. In a busy restaurant, the sommelier having to describe perhaps an average of three or four wines to each table might rely on just a handful of key words such as light, dry, crisp, full, firm, round, smooth, one or two synonyms for smell, along with the occasional anecdote. The quality of the wines being presented also has an effect on length: a range of plonk is less likely to inspire you than a set of top Cabernet Sauvignon wines from around the world.

In terms of their quality, the length of tasting notes is not that important. Indeed the same wine can be extremely well described either in just a few words, bullet-point style, or by a whole paragraph of several sentences. Bear in mind, however, that while long descriptions can convey more information, they can also result in confusion.

Content, on the other hand, is what makes a tasting note interesting and useful, or boring and pointless. Notes can be written on an analytical basis or with the intention of conveying a specific idea with much more scope for interpretation.

Analytical tasting notes focus primarily on the wines, and the tasters will try to be as objective as they possibly can. Wine-makers tasting several barrels of their unfinished wines will write fairly terse descriptions, making sure that their notes cover all the appropriate aspects of the wines. The same applies to wine buyers, wine merchants, sommeliers or journalists when they are buying or selecting wines. Naturally they will not look at the wines in exactly the same way and their comments on the same wines might differ. Nevertheless their philosophy will be the same. Relevance and precision will no doubt dominate their thinking. Bare analytical tasting notes are often principally for the tasters' own use and therefore do not need any sort of embellishment. But when tasters have to consider not just the wines but also the people who will drink them, the philosophy behind the tasting notes might change significantly.

Tasting notes containing a high proportion of interpretation may be influenced by a commercial angle, in which case they will probably accentuate the best aspects of the wines and ignore their more ordinary sides. That is not to say that such descriptions are untrue, but that they may be diverting the consumers' attention from the complete wine picture. Wine buyers for shops or restaurants will sometimes buy a wine because it fills a gap (a good price point) or because of its originality (an unknown grape or a new wine area), even though its quality, while perfectly

acceptable, might be fairly average. Describing the wine on a list or directly to consumers, words such as 'interesting' or 'different' will be used to supplement the one or two adjectives used to transmit a sense of its taste. Sometimes more is said of what the wine is not than of what it is: for example, 'a very different wine, which does not smell like an exotic fruit salad or an infusion of new oak, but which has an interesting character of its own; excellent with seafood'! Of course not all commercial tasting notes are waffle like this, but it is worth bearing in mind that only the positive sides of the wines are likely to be emphasised.

However this should not always be looked on with suspicion; for instance serious wine merchants have very few dud wines on their lists and their customers want to read exciting things on the many superb wines they stock. Wine merchants such as John Armit, Bibendum, Yapp Brothers or the Wine Society have very informative wine lists which are truly a pleasure to read, even if you are not in the mood for buying, they give you the same tingle of excitement that children have in a toy shop.

With or without a commercial angle, tasting notes are often written in an artistic, poetic or entertaining style, leading on occasion to some unusual words or eccentric descriptions. Examples such as 'a wheelbarrow full of ugli fruit' by Jilly Goolden, smelling of 'hamster cages' by Giles MacDonogh, 'reminiscent of a sumo wrestler's thighs' (I do not know the author) have become real classics and have made some wine experts and wine lovers complain vehemently against that approach, often referred to it as the fruit-salad school of wine description (or the bubble-gum school). The reproach is that it lays the whole business of wine-tasting open to ridicule.

Jilly Goolden, one of those at whom the finger is often pointed, gives her explanation in her book *The Taste of Wine* (1994):

> You only have to read a couple of lines of the tasting notes in this book to realise that I am a committed-up-to-the-eyebrows pupil of the bubble-gum school. I always feel cheated when I find that the taste of a wine is simply not described in a book devoted to the subject (and it virtually never is). What good is, and I quote, 'elegant and close knit, perky and slightly assertive. Charming and definitively well bred?' It could be a thumb-nail sketch of the Royal family [...] a fat lot it tells you about the taste of a particular wine (it was a Champagne, as it happens). As far as I am concerned, the taste is the crux of the whole matter so, for my purposes, I try to describe it as best I can so that anyone reading the notes can imagine what the wine is like.

Even if her over-the-top style can be a bit exasperating, on many occasions I do agree with quite a lot of Jilly Goolden's views. Some traditionalists would have it that only words such as finesse, breed, class, balance or complexity have a place in the world of wine vocabulary. There is nothing wrong with those words but I think they should be used in preference as summing-up expressions after a more descriptive vocabulary. Indeed I think tasters really should attempt to describe the smells from a glass of wine.

Descriptions such as the far fetched examples given earlier are perfectly valid if they are for the tasters' own use. We all have a unique perception of our surroundings, as well as harbouring individual likes and dislikes, however, I do think that unless you are trying to be funny or deliberately provocative, fanciful descriptions are of little use to other tasters. They are fine in the mouths of TV pundits such as Jilly Goolden and Oz Clarke who have to an audience to entertain, but who also have an extensive knowledge of wine so deserve to be taken seriously and forgiven a bit of eccentricity, but they can fall rather flat in the mouths of others.

Some tasters do not just stop at the use of fanciful words with regard to the smell of wine but turn the whole tasting note upside down. Rather like the hilarious classic from James Thurber's cartoon: 'It's a naïve domestic Burgundy, with no great breeding, but I

think you'll be amused by its presumption.'

In my opinion smells for each wine should be described as far as possible using comparisons with popular foods, flowers or other familiar substances. The occasional oddity is fine but only if used sparingly.

During a visit to the Chablis area, more than ten years ago, I remember listening to Patrick Pages, a French sommelier/restaurateur. Commenting on a set of Chablis to a large audience, mainly from the wine trade, he described with great imagination the wonderful aromas of those wines; for instance, he compared one particular smell he was getting to those found in his grandmother's kitchen when she was cooking fruit to make jam. His descriptions were always wrapped in this sort of lyricism, but always with some extra dimension: not just the jam but also Grandma's presence. A bit overdone, perhaps, but beautiful to listen to and it really made you want to drink those wines.

The number of smells used to describe a wine should not be too numerous as this can be counter-productive. Imagine if I invited you for dinner at my home and I told you that my wife Nina was planning a grilled sea bass with olive oil, served with some pan-fried courgettes and tomatoes; it might or might not appeal to you but at least you would have a fairly good idea of what flavours to expect. Now imagine if I told you that the same sea bass was to be marinated in white wine, coconut milk, lime juice, ginger, coriander, celery, wild mushroom and some honey: it might turn out to be a good dish but I doubt if you would have a clear idea on which flavours to expect.

In the book *La Dégustation* edited by the *Journal International des Sciences de la Vigne et du Vin* in 1999 there is a report based on the conclusions of the work carried out by some Australian researchers measuring the capacity of trained subjects and experts (perfumers) to identify aromas in specially created mixes. The result showed that none of the people involved in the test could identify more than four aromas. This led to the following comment on the tasting descriptions regularly found around us: 'Not only can the taster not improve his or her performance but the performances which are generally displayed in tasting commentaries are already way above actual human abilities!'

David Apel and Clas Robert Wulff, two senior perfumers working with Fragrance Resources, explained to me that they regularly train their nose by trying to recognise some specific single aroma that they regularly use in combination to create new perfumes or modify existing ones. However they pointed out that, even with their constant training, aroma recognition is not an exact science and for instance trying to assess what was in the blend of a competitor's perfume was far from simple, and failures were quite common.

It is probably fair to say that tasting notes are received by two types of consumers. On one hand are those who are continually bemused to hear that a wine can smell of apple, rose, chocolate, tobacco, leather or petrol; isn't wine made from grapes? And on the other hand, there are those who expect any wine to have a very recognisable smell character, be it of banana, violet, toffee, ginger or lanolin. The reality lies very much in between these two points of view. Because the odour molecules found in many wines can be chemically similar to a wide range of products. It is true that many wines do smell like something else (Sauvignon Blanc and gooseberry is a perfect example), however in many cases the smell encountered in a wine is far from being an exact copy of a familiar product. It might only vaguely resemble it. After all, the possibilities in chemical wine smell constitutions are endless, which means that on occasion the description used is based on a sensation partly recognised and partly imagined. Your strawberry smell may be my raspberry smell or the redcurrant of the taster next to us. In fact sometimes if you read the tasting notes of a group of tasters on a particular example you could seriously question that they had all tasted the same wine. Nevertheless, this should not horrify outsiders. During a tasting session tasters are genuinely trying to put a name to each smell encountered, but if it proves impossible they will tag the unidentified smell with whatever they think is closest in character. Ironically this desire for exactitude in wines with difficult odours can render the wine description more confusing, except to its author. We should not lose sight of the fact that it does not matter how good a tasting note is, it is a very personal matter and therefore can never be completely understood by someone else.

When describing a wine myself I try to stick to two smells, a dominant one and what I call a supportive one, and only when I am particularly inspired might I add a third one. The dominant one might be a single smell such as lychee, honey or blackcurrant, and if less distinctive it may be just a group of smells such as tropical fruit or flowers. The same is true of the second smell, so I might choose: passionfruit and herbaceous; tropical fruit and vanilla; or spice and red fruit. While I agree that describing the nose of a wine by two groups of smells rather than more specific ones (strawberry rather than red fruit), might not be very informative, remember that some wines are simply not very expressive. The key is to be honest with yourself; it is easy to pinpoint smells for some wines but with others you get only a vague impression.

Describing the smell of a wine is an important aspect of tasting notes, but it is not the only one. Quite often enthusiasts of the fruit-salad school of wine-tasting come up with numerous descriptions of the aroma, but forget to tell us much about how the wine feels in the mouth. As a sommelier, having long experience of dealing directly with consumers, I notice that, in general, the first thing diners want to know about a wine is if it is dry or not so dry, crisp or smooth, light or full. In other words how it will feel in the mouth, and only then are they interested in whether it is spicy, oaky, flowery or blackcurranty. While I have no direct experience, I suspect that the same is true of customers in a wine shop.

As we have already seen, oral tasting commentaries, in a restaurant or shop, are normally quite brief, so it is

important that they are both interesting and informative. A short description such as 'full and velvety with gorgeous plummy flavours' or 'fresh and crisp, packed with gooseberry and passion fruit flavours', possibly with some short details on the winery or the wine-makers to lighten the chat, such as 'the vineyard is organically farmed' or 'Mr X the wine-maker does not like using new oak' is usually enough, unless of course the customer is a real enthusiast and asks for more information. Unfortunately too often a wine is just described with a meaningless 'very nice' and not much else. We have all been guilty of such banalities of course, myself included; after all when you work with a great number of wines you can occasionally be caught off guard with a wine you haven't tasted for a long time. However it is worth trying to prevent this happening. If you really cannot say much about a wine, then it is better to come clean and admit that you are not really sure how it tastes at the moment.

In some restaurants tasting notes are sometimes added to the wine list. Either short ones at the head of a category, as for example 'Firm and full' under which you might see a range of young Cabernet Sauvignon or Barolo wines listed, or individual tasting notes for each wine on the list. Both approaches, if done with care, can work extremely well. The wine list of the Old Bridge at Huntingdon near Cambridge, selected and written by Master of Wine and proprietor John Hoskins, skilfully combines both systems and is well selected, witty and informative; apart from the fact that there are no descriptive headings, the same can be said of the list at the Wykeham Arms in Winchester compiled by wine lover Graeme Jameson.

The great advantages of wine lists with notes are that customers have some instant information on the taste of the wines, can take longer to make their decision and, if they are a bit shy, do not have to risk been sneered at by a supercilious sommelier (I promise we are not all like that!). However the quality of the tasting notes is not always very high. And when notes are given for each wine, on a very large wine list the descriptions can become repetitive and make reading the list long and tedious. Furthermore, for a very large list, I doubt whether all the wines are tasted regularly and therefore if all the notes are accurate, or if they are are stale ramblings disguised by technical jargon. My advice for a restaurateur in charge of a large list who wants it to contain tasting notes is to add them for just a fraction of the wines but to change the wines described regularly. So the list could open with a two- or three-page selection of wines from different styles and price brackets fully described, followed by the rest of the list without notes.

A wine taster for whom I have a great deal of admiration and who in my opinion has achieved the right mix of description with his tasting notes is the American Stephen Tanzer in his newsletter, *Stephen Tanzer's International Wine Cellar* to which my friend Richard Lashbrook MW recently introduced me. From reading his comments and observing the ratings Stephen gives wines, it is evident that he has a very good palate and is also an excellent communicator. He manages to convey to the reader a real feel for the wines, in terms of their smells, flavours and structure, without recourse to too many strange words.

The American wine magazine *Wine X* has specialised in a completely unconventional wine language. And why not? If it is done with good sense and good humour, it is more fun than listening to a bunch of wine snobs delivering some tedious nonsense. The following are typical examples from *Wine X*:

Brutocao Chardonnay 1997, Bliss Vineyard, Mendocino California: *'Like the movie* A Clockwork Orange, *stylistic, toasted and nuts.'*

Guenoc Zinfandel 1997, California: *'Like Sharon Stone in a pair of Tony Lama boots – sweet spice, leather and well built.'*

Talking of unconventional wine language, I have to confess that at times I have used perfectly conventional wine language to describe something other than wine. When my partner Robin Hutson and I first opened the Hotel du Vin in Winchester we were both very hands-on, working all sort of hours, sometimes being waiter/ head waiter/sommelier all at once, as well as porter, receptionist, night porter and even, on rare occasions, helping in the kitchen. (Now you are more likely to find Robin smoking one of the best Cuban cigars and me enjoying a glass of 'Super Tuscan' wine!) So during our few quiet moments, like two schoolboys looking for mischief, we would discreetly glance at the female clientele of the restaurant and comment on their figures in wine-related terms. 'Did you see table 8? Definitely a good Merlot, ripe and smooth.' 'What about the brunette in the left-hand corner, more like a Chablis, lean and crisp?' 'Oh yes, and a grand cru at that. Outraged feminist readers should take comfort from the fact that the tables were turned on me. At my wedding Robin, during his speech as my best man, compared me to a slightly overripe bottle of wine of possibly good cru bourgeois quality. Moi! Cru bourgeois? I always thought I was first growth material!

ABBREVIATED TASTING NOTES

During big wine tastings, organised by wine merchants or generic bodies, or at wine fairs, tasters have an opportunity to sample a very large number of wines on the same day. These are the perfect occasions on which to discover interesting wines or compare similar ones. However, because of the surrounding noise, the often slightly cramped environment, the disturbance from meeting friends or colleagues and the fact that it is the norm to use the same glass over and over again, tasting conditions (normally standing up) are not ideally suited for total concentration or the assessing of wines with great precision. In fact, I find it is easier to try to write a short profile of the major aspects of each wine rather than to attempt a long, thorough description (as shown in chapter 3 pages 54–79). Also, writing hundreds of words while standing up with a glass in hand can quickly become tedious.

For large tastings like these, I approach the notes in a different way. I have therefore designed two systems: one uses a code that gives a reasonable picture of the wine and also answers certain questions about it, the other is what I call the 'five-word minimum description'. The latter is less complete than the code system but more fun, albeit less precise. Of course neither system is definitive and can easily be amended to suit the aims of different tasters, but whatever the final system chosen, the taster should stick to it fairly rigorously so as to feel at ease with it.

In most cases at large tastings, tasters know the wines' identity (grape(s), origin, vintage, producer) and price. Therefore the main purpose of the exercise is to see if and how the wine matches, exceeds or fails to approach a set of known standards. In the case of an unfamiliar style of wine, the tasters will use those wines to start establishing their own standards.

JOHN HARVEY

tasting notes in code

This system examines twelve aspects of each wine, always the same and always in the same order. The choice for each aspect is deliberately narrow. Indeed I think that in such circumstances, concentrating on just a few possibilities is less confusing and allows the taster to remain sharply focused throughout the tasting.

1 GENERAL APPEARANCE

A straightforward assessment, for which most wines should receive a 'normal' rating.

N = Normal

D = Deep for a very intense appearance

P = Pale for a very light appearance

O = Odd-looking, too old (for the vintage) or strange (e.g. pinkish for a white wine)

Sections 2–4 give a quick round-up of the nose, with a rating for its intensity, two distinctive smells and a verdict on both its nature and quality.

2 EXPRESSION

P = Positive

S = Strong

R = Reserved

W = Weak

C = Closed

3 SMELL

Leading Role = the strongest smell, either a group or an individual one

Supporting Role = the second strongest smell, also a group or an individual one

4 NATURE AND QUALITY

The symbols can be supplemented by a word of explanation, especially in the case of WM (Wine-making) such as cold fermentation, carbonic maceration, flor. The minus or plus signs are of course rating short cuts for quality.

V = Varietal (V-, V, V+)

WM = Wine-making (WM-, WM, WM+)

R = Regional (R-, R, R+)

DR = Development Reductive (DR-, DR, DR+)

DO = Development Oxidative (DO-, DO, DO+)

In sections 5–7 the tasters assess the body of each wine, its structure with a minus-equal-plus scale to incorporate in part the quality of both its texture and balance and its length. The quality of a wine's structure is linked to its texture, which in turn partly gives an answer on its overall balance. So I assess the structure and simply add a very basic quality rating similar to the one used under nature and quality of the nose section.

Because the aim of my coding is to be rapid and economical, the mouth aromas, which I personally refer to as flavours (strictly speaking flavours are more than just mouth aromas; see the section on judging flavour in chapter 5 page 133), are not assessed as they are fairly similar to the smells perceived on the nose.

5 BODY

T = Thin

L = Light

MW = Middle-Weight

FB = Full-Bodied

H = Heavy

6 STRUCTURE, TEXTURE, BALANCE

C = Coarse

S = Solid (S-, S, S+)

T = Tight (T-, T, T+)

J = Juicy (J-, J, J+)

Su = Supple (Su-, Su, Su+)

R = Round (R-, R, R+)

F = Flat

7 LENGTH

BL = Beautiful and Long

N = Nice

I = Indifferent

U = Unpleasant

In sections 8 to 12 the tasters decided whether the wines are representative of a grape or an area; if they will keep, need drinking now or are past their best; if the wines represent good value for money or not; how much they personally like the wines; and finally their objective appraisal as to the overall quality of the wines.

8 TYPICITY

Some wines display the character of either the grape or the wine area so well that they are said to be typical. For wines made from little-known grape varieties or in unproven areas, typicalness does not yet apply, which is why I have given the Non-applicable rating.

A = Archetype

L = Loose

I = Idiosyncratic

NA = Non-applicable

9 Potential

N = Now

NT = Now and Tomorrow

T = Tomorrow

Y = Yesterday

10 VALUE FOR MONEY

I tend to give an irrelevant rating to a wine that is overall of high quality, high reputation and very expensive (but not too much over the market price).

Normally they are rare collectors' wines and their price is principally dictated by demand so I see no point in rating their value for money. Would a painting by Bacon, Monet or Picasso be worth its market price on the basis of the quality of the painting alone? Difficult to answer and frankly irrelevant as the demand far outweighs the supply.

G = Great

F = Fair

P = Poor

I = Irrelevant

11 PERSONAL PREFERENCE

It is important to separate this aspect from the next one. After all, just as you can like a simple tune knowing it is not great music, so you can like a simple wine. You need to be conscious of its true quality however.

L = Love it

E = Enjoy it

OK = Slight Enjoyment

D = Dislike it

12 OBJECTIVE EVALUATION

S = Seriously Good Quality

R = Regular Quality

E = Easy Drinking Quality

B = Boring

C = Common

conclusion

In chapter 5 when describing my system, I explained that I did not allocate any marks for an overall evaluation of a wine. When you score a wine you should only be concerned with one aspect – absolute quality, which is indicated by adding up the marks from the separate sections (appearance, nose, palate : structure, flavour, balance, length). When you are describing a wine (see chapters 3 and 6) you are concerned with other factors (such as overall style, value for money) in addition to absolute quality. Therefore you do require a final section to sum up all of the wine's aspects.

1 General Appearance	N, D, P, O
2 Expression	P, S, R, W, C
3 Odour	Leading role + Supporting role
4 Nature and Quality	V (-,=,+), WM (-,=,+), R (-,=,+), DR (-,=,+), DO (-,=,+)
5 Body	T, L, MW, FB, H
6 Structure, Texture , Balance	C, S (-,=,+), T (-,=,+), J (-,=,+), Su (-,=,+), R (-,=,+), F
7 Length	BL, N, I, U

8 Typicity	A, L, I, NA
9 Potential	N, NT, T, Y
10 Value for Money	G, F, P, I
11 Personal Preference	L, E, OK, D
12 Objective Evaluation	S, R, E, B, C

EXAMPLES:

A Chardonnay received the following assessment:

N/S, tropical fruit and vanilla, WM/MW, J, N/A, N, F, E, R

A Pinot Noir received the following assessment:

N/P, bitter cherry and gamey, R+/MW, Su+, BL/A, NT, I, L, S

The five-word minimum description

The idea behind this method is to concentrate only on the most useful information of a wine's aspect. Those criteria might not be exactly the same for every taster but they should not be too different either. Whereas I feel that five words is a minimum description, on occasion six, seven or even more might be necessary, so let's not be too strict.

My preference is to omit the appearance (can be the sixth or seventh word if really special) and to focus directly on the style (first word), and character (second word) of the nose; then the weight (third word) and the mouthfeel (fourth word) of the palate followed by a general impression (fifth word).

The vocabulary is similar to that of other wine-tasting notes systems we have seen, complemented by a few more colourful words. In fact, here it is more of a wine caricature we are trying to obtain. Because the emphasis is on a very limited number of aspects, it inevitably gives a slightly distorted picture of the wine. Nevertheless if done seriously it should still reflect a wine's taste and quality. After all, caricatures of famous people sometimes look better than a photograph.

VOCABULARY

1 Style (nose) (if not faulty)

Extrovert: artificial, synthetic, manufactured, obvious, assertive, exuberant, fruit-driven, perfumed, pure.

Reserved: bland, simple, straightforward, restrained, fragrant, complex.

2 Character (nose)

Note the dominant odour, whether an individual one (e.g. pineapple) or a group (e.g. fresh flowers). Of course you might want to use two words in this section (e.g. pineapple, vanilla), which is fine

3 Weight (palate)

Watery, diluted, thin, lean, light, middle-weight, full-bodied, blockbuster, massive, heavy.

4 Mouthfeel (palate)

Negative: coarse, green, sharp, hard, harsh, rough, tough, chewy, austere, severe, loose, flat, flabby, syrupy, cloying.

Positive: solid, firm, ample, compact, steely, robust, fleshy, tight, crisp, close-knit, juicy, fresh, lively, supple, delicate, creamy, silky, soft, round, fat, smooth, rich, velvety, luscious, opulent.

5 General impressions (verdict)

Do not forget to take into consideration the length of the wine in this section.

From negative to positive: faulty, nasty, real plonk, fair jug wine, quaffing or easy-drinking, good commercial style, enjoyable, lovely, gorgeous, delicious, sensational.

Can be supplemented with (if you need a sixth word): disappointing, surprising, as expected.

As examples, my recent description of a disappointing Pinot Noir was: assertive, vegetal, middle-weight, chewy, real plonk; but my five words of description for an excellent Marsanne wine were fragrant, anis, full-bodied, luscious, gorgeous

Whatever words you choose to use, make sure you cover the major aspects (at least smell, mouthfeel and overall impression), that your choice of words is relevant and that you do not contradict yourself: crisp and round?; tough and supple?; complex, silky, quaffing?; manufactured, diluted, gorgeous? The last two examples are a bit extreme but it is not unusual to see tasting notes with similar contradictions!

Finally, for every tasting note you write, be it a full description, just a few words or in code, you need to date it. Indeed, when reading a tasting note about a fifteen-year-old wine, it is essential to know if the description was made when the wine was one, five, ten or fifteen years old.

chapter 7

blind tasting

Blind tasting is to wine-tasting what the triple axel is to figure skating: the ultimate thrill! Although only one aspect of wine-tasting, it is nevertheless one of the most fascinating. Unidentified wines are given to tasters who must attempt to ascertain the grape(s), the origin and the vintage of each wine.

In order to differentiate between blind tasting for quality grading (partly identified wines) and blind tasting for wine identification (completely unidentified wines) the former is increasingly referred to as a 'single blind tasting' and the latter as a 'double blind tasting'. In the first case the purpose is to assess and rank the wines, as is done in wine shows, while in the second case it is the tasters who are assessed to judge their competence, as in Master of Wine examinations or sommelier competitions.

When blind tasting is mentioned it means only one thing for most people: a guessing game! No information at all is provided. The wine could be made from a single grape variety or several, and could have been produced anywhere in the world; it is up to you to find the correct answer. What could be more exciting than witnessing grown adults torturing themselves over a glass of wine? But beware: this exercise can have a devastating effect on your self-esteem. Maybe people from the wine trade go through these masochistic sessions simply as a way of apologising for all the marvellous bottles we are so often blessed to sample.

TWO APPROACHES TO BLIND TASTING

There are two different approaches to try to beat the odds. On occasion both can lead to spectacular results.

The first method is simply recognising the wine in front of you. Like Archimedes in his bath you have had a brainwave. Lucky you! An inspiration like this has been provoked by what you can remember of all the wines you have previously drunk. Indeed a good memory is central to this system since you can only recall the wines or wine styles you have tasted before. Therefore if you are confronted with something completely new to you, this technique alone will not be of much help. Furthermore, having tasted a wine before is no guarantee that you will identify it again, unless you have tasted it very recently, you taste it regularly, or it is a highly rare and unusual wine that has stuck in your memory.

If you intend to tackle blind tasting this way bear in mind that you are not in command. There is nothing more frustrating than thinking you know the wine, its name is on the tip of your tongue, but you are unable to retrieve it! You are left feeling completely helpless. Mind you, if you have reached that stage with this method you are not doing so badly; more often than not you will simply not have a clue.

As a method, simple recognition is too passive. It can sometimes work, and, like most tasters, the first thing I do when confronted with a set of unknown wines is to put my nose quickly into each glass hoping to find a few 'bankers' (jargon meaning a wine that is usually easy to detect thanks to its specific character e.g. Marlborough Sauvignon Blanc or traditional red Rioja). If no bright idea emerges quickly I do not persist with that system, but move on to the second. Even if I think I might have uncovered the answers I still go through the second process as a back-up.

For plan number two you are going to transform yourself into a Sherlock Holmes or Hercule Poirot. Like the famous detectives you will be conducting an investigation, but instead of looking for a culprit you will be trying to unmask the identity of a wine.

The principles are similar. and very simple: first you collect as much information as you possibly can, then you dissect it rationally. Dead simple really! The only difference is that the success rate somehow never seems to match that of our two detectives.

Unlike the first method in which you rely on memory alone, you have to be extremely thorough in your observations and open-minded in your thinking. It can be rather slow, hard work.

Much more than in the first system you must know pretty well what to look for in a wine to have a real chance. Since evaluation plays a great part you must at least have a sound knowledge of the major grape varieties, a fair idea of the climatic and environmental conditions of the principal wine-producing regions, a

basic understanding of grape growing and wine-making and finally have tasted a wide range of wines.

It will not take you too long to reach a decent level of wine appreciation. Start by concentrating your wine-tasting on the noble grape varieties and classic wine-producing areas (New World and Old World). When tasting focus on the main elements of each wine and try to grasp what differentiates the principal styles of wine. If you know a competent taster ask for a bit of guidance and read about wine to deepen your understanding.

Your level of success will rest on your observational skills and on how well you interpret those observations. The idea is that by the end of the tasting the precious information you have collected will allow you, first of all, to eliminate certain options in order to narrow down the field and then enable you to make your final choice. It is rather like gathering material in two files: one building up the case for what the wine could not possibly be and the other for what the wine might be. The key to success is that these two files do not contradict each other and that they provide you with enough elements on which to make a final decision.

The way to put these principles into practice is to answer these questions methodically and thoroughly:

A) What does the appearance of this wine tell us?

B) What does the nose of this wine tell us?

C) What does the palate of this wine tell us?

For each of these questions try to link your observations to the main elements of a wine's identity i.e.: the grape(s), the origin, age/maturity, production methods and quality level. Those observations for each question can only give you part of the overall answer. For instance the appearance of the wine is unlikely to tell you the name of the grape but it might give you an idea as to the maturity of the wine. It is the sum of all your observations that will lead to the solution.

BLIND TASTING A WHITE WINE

Let's put this theory into practice. Here is a white wine with the following tasting notes:

> Very limpid and star bright, pale green-yellow, small number of tiny bubbles on the rim, quite fluid.
> Clean nose, weak intensity, not aromatic, just very slightly fruity and a touch sherbety, no smell of new oak detectable.
> Dry, medium alcohol, moderate acidity, light body, loose but not flabby, could do with a bit of crispness, simple flavours with little definition, just balanced, clean but indifferent finish.
> Overall certainly not unpleasant but lacking in any sort of character, quaffing wine that will not improve.

What do these notes tell us?

Appearance: the pale colour seems to indicate that this wine was not made from grapes grown in very warm conditions and it most probably removes the possibility of having been matured in new oak. The green-yellow colour and, to a lesser extent, the visible CO_2 are two factors that should direct us towards a young wine. Due to the fairly fluid aspect of the wine we should not expect very high alcohol or much residual sugar in the wine.

Nose: the weak intensity should rule out any aromatic grape variety. The clean nose and fruit aromas, albeit very slight, suggest technically competent wine-making and support the impression of youthfulness. In fact the sherbety notes would suggest a wine fermented at cool temperatures. The lack of new oak ageing is confirmed by the absence of any toasty/vanilla smells. The simple but moderate character is fairly typical of a certain style of mass-produced wine.

Palate: there are no really obvious properties here, such as a small amount of residual sugar left in the wine, or a naturally high acidity or even a richness in texture that can help us to recognise a particular wine style or identify the grape variety. The wine is unlikely to come from a cool climate area, as it would again have more acidity. Nevertheless the lightness in body eliminates a warm climate too. In addition to its light body the combination of a rather loose structure, a weak concentration of flavour and the indifferent finish tend to indicate a wine produced from fairly modest raw materials, most probably a high-yielding vineyard. Your deductions at this point might be along the following lines:

Grape: the modest character on the nose and the lack of any distinctive features on the palate can only tell us that it is not made from one of the noble grape varieties, thus making it difficult to pinpoint one in particular. Consequently to identify the grape(s), information not directly related to its taste will be required.

Origin: within the climatic parameters observed (neither cool nor very warm) Europe would be a better bet than many New World wine areas, but the fact that no regional characteristic is manifest means that the possibilities remain wide open, so to uncover the origin we need to consider information from other sections.

Production: the combination of a spotless appearance and some simple but rather diluted flavours is often an indication of an ordinary wine (high yields) submitted to a large amount of manipulation (e.g. cold stabilisation, tight filtration). The only useful pieces of information evident seem to be that the wine was cold fermented (sherbet smell) and not matured in new oak.

Maturity: the impression of youth evident from the wine's appearance is supported by the light but irrefutable touch of fruit on the nose. Because of its limited attributes the wine should not be kept for ageing but consumed in the coming weeks (or even days!).

Style and quality: its somewhat uninspiring style (simple flavours, weak structure, ordinary length) puts this wine firmly in the inexpensive commercial band of wine retailing, very much in the style of old-fashioned European big brands or modest generic appellations. However because of its total dryness, a generic appellation is more likely as many old-fashioned big brands often have a little residual sugar left in to hide any slight touch of bitterness.

Final conclusion: when all these considerations are put together, opting for an Italian wine such as a one- or two-year-old basic Soave (sound, neutral, light, white wine) would not seem illogical. Tasting a top Soave from Anselmi, Inama or Pieropan would be a completely different experience, a real treat!

The original tasting notes could have fitted numerous wines, so if you had decided on another simple, neutral style of wine, such as a Fendant of ordinary quality from Switzerland or an inexpensive South African Chenin Blanc you would not have been too far from the correct result.

BLIND TASTING A RED WINE

Let's repeat the exercise with a red wine which has the following tasting notes:

> Opaque, bright, full ruby red with just a hint of purple/pink on the rim, no CO_2 visible, quite viscous with heavy tears.
> Clean, powerful nose of very ripe blackcurrant and black cherry, almost jammy, but elegantly supported by some meaty and tobacco notes, subtle new oak smell detectable but very well integrated.
> Dry, high alcohol but not burning, moderate but adequate acidity, rich in smooth tannins, full-bodied, a real blockbuster, round and opulent structure, packed with appealing flavours similar to those picked up on the nose with maybe an additional leathery touch, perfectly balanced in spite of the high alcohol, beautiful and long finish.
> Overall: a splendid wine of ageing potential, blessed with many attributes giving the wine a lot of character.

What do these notes tell us?:

Appearance: the highly saturated colour indicates a wine from a grape variety with a skin rich in colour pigments and harvested when very ripe, definitely not from a coolish climate; furthermore it suggests that the wine has only been lightly filtered, if at all. The full

ruby colour with just a small purple/pinkish rim indicates a relatively immature wine. Because of the pronounced viscosity, a full-bodied wine high in alcohol should be expected.

Nose: the powerful and expressive character on the nose reveals a noble grape variety. The blackcurrant and black cherry smells suggest Cabernet Sauvignon, quite possibly Merlot or even perhaps Syrah/Shiraz. The jammy touch confirms the good level of ripeness in the grapes at harvest time. The excellent integration of the smell of new oak is a sign of high-quality wine-making. Furthermore the fact that no real spicy or strong coconut/vanilla odours are detected suggests that French rather than American oak has been used. In spite of its youth, the meaty and tobacco smells seem to imply a wine that is starting to evolve.

Palate: the high level of tannins, albeit very ripe in style, is an additional pointer for the Cabernet Sauvignon grape. The high alcohol content, the moderate acidity and the smoothness of tannins are clear indicators of a warm climate. However, the superb quality of the flavours is not synonymous with an excessively warm climate. The round and opulent structure, coupled with the rich concentration of flavours denote high-quality production values, such as controlled yields in the vineyard and careful maturation with minimum handling. The excellent balance and the beautiful long finish confirm we are dealing with a wine of premium quality, therefore it is most probably from a prestigious wine area.

Your deductions at this stage might be along the following lines:

Grape: the deep colour, plentiful tannins, ample structure and body, but above all the very characteristic blackcurrant-dominated smell make Cabernet Sauvignon a serious probability. Merlot could be considered but a blackcurrant flavour is less common, especially in the ripest examples, which are normally plummier. Regarding Syrah/Shiraz, French Syrah wines would probably have more gamey and peppery flavours and would not be so opulent in structure, whereas from Australian Shiraz we could anticipate slightly sweeter fruit flavours with some chocolate undertones. So Cabernet Sauvignon must be the best option.

Origin: because of its specific colour, powerful structure and the superb quality of its flavours, we can establish that it is from a fairly warm area (most probably eliminating Bordeaux) producing high-quality wines. Therefore Australia (e.g. Coonowarra, although on the cool side of warm, Margaret River, Mclaren Vale), California (e.g. Napa, Sonoma, Santa Cruz Mountains), Chile (Maipo), South Africa (Stellenbosch), and also Tuscany (Bolgheri) seem to be among the contenders. However, a very full body and such an opulent structure are slightly less common in Cabernet Sauvignon wines from Chile, South Africa and Tuscany. So we are left with areas of Australia or California to choose from. We should probably disregard Australia as minty flavours, a familiar aspect of many Australian Cabernet Sauvignon wines, could have been expected (although stronger in wines from Victoria, they are often slightly present in those from other regions). Some spiciness or coconut/vanilla smells are also common due to the more customary use of American oak in their top Cabernet wines. California produces many high-quality blockbuster Cabernet Sauvignon wines, especially the Napa Valley area, which has many boutique wineries specialising in this style, so that is a logical option.

Production: fullness both in the colour and the body of the wine, wonderful mouthfeel, and powerful but magnificent smells and flavours can only be produced as a result of maximum care at the vineyard (restricted yields and great attention to care of the grapes) and total dedication to the wine-making process (minimum handling but constant monitoring). In fact because of its level of extraction (colour, body, etc.) it is possible that the wine has been given an extended time of skin maceration during fermentation and quite probably it has been neither filtered nor fined, or only very slightly. The superb ripeness of the tannin, coupled with the beautiful flavours suggest that the wine has been matured in new oak barrels (most probably French as it is more subdued) for between sixteen and twenty-four months in a perfectly controlled oxidative state, with regular topping-up of the barrels and periodic racking (three to four times a year, which would also explain the brightness of such a deep-coloured wine).

Maturity: it is quite obvious that the wine is still immature (bright ruby colour, small purple/pinkish rim, plenty of fruit on the nose); nevertheless the smells are not just fruit and some appealing meaty and tobacco odours in the background are more consistent with a wine that has just lost its exuberant youth and is probably four to six years old. In spite of its opulent structure, the intensity of the tannin leads one to expect a wine with a long ageing potential and the full concentration of flavours should guarantee that it will not dry out for several years.

Style and quality: its extremely generous complexion and its powerful but distinctive smells place this wine in a modern style of high-quality wine-making very popular with influential wine critics (especially American ones). This wine, with its appealing colour, attractive smells, wonderful mouthfeel, superb balance and beautiful long finish can only be described as outstanding.

Final conclusion: Cabernet Sauvignon, Napa Valley, four to six years old, high-quality wine for keeping, top winery.

With experience and regular practice, coming that close to identifying a wine is by no means an impossible feat. In addition, an expressive wine like that Napa Valley Cabernet Sauvignon provides you with adequate information to enable you to succeed in your reasoning. However, mistakes are easily made, even by the most experienced tasters.

Although, this may all seem rather simple and straightforward, in practice it can prove rather more complex. Not only will you have days of good and bad form but also you cannot take as an absolute certainty the taste of wines from any given area. Generalisations are helpful, but you need to be flexible and allow for exceptions. As Robert Joseph put it, not every Swede is blond and not every Cabernet Sauvignon wine has an aroma of blackcurrant! Furthermore, some wine areas seem to be more consistent in their flavour profile than others. Most tasters will have a pretty clear idea of what to expect from a classic Médoc classed growth but I am not so sure that they could say the same of a red Châteauneuf du Pape.

It is crucial to understand that trends in wine change, and technology never stops progressing. Wine-producing methods change with the times so that what is relevant today may not be so in the future. What we might regard as the taste of a typical Californian Chardonnay or a classic Barossa Shiraz today might be different in ten years' time. A good illustration is found in Bordeaux wine from the right bank of the Garonne river, where the influence of oenologist Michel Rolland, with his insistence on both full ripeness and great extraction of colour, has greatly changed the style of the area's wines in the 1990s. If you want to stand a chance in blind tastings you must keep abreast of what is happening in the wine world!

Think laterally and evaluate every possibility; in particular, reflect on the following:

The effects of grape(s): smell profile, body and mouthfeel (in particular levels of alcohol, acidity and tannin), and finally its intrinsic quality.

The effects of both climatic conditions and vintage

conditions: cold, cool, temperate, warm, hot, rainy, late harvest, botrytis influencing the level of alcohol, acidity, sugar, ripeness of tannin, flavour profile.

The effects of vineyard management: yield, ripeness, botrytis, eiswein influencing flavour, body and mouthfeel.

The effects of wine-making: protective, reductive, oxidative. Mostly for white wine: skin contact (and length of), whole bunch pressing, flavour-enhancing yeasts, cold fermentation, malolactic, less stirring, yeast autolysis, flor, cold stabilisation, new oak ageing, residual sugar, fortification, sterile filtration, level of SO_2. Mostly for red wines: flavour-enhancing yeasts, de-stemming or not, whole bunches or crushing, cap management (manner and length of maceration), carbonic maceration, free-run wine and press wine, must or wine concentration/extraction, new oak ageing, racking, filtration, fining, fortification level of volatile acidity. These all influence the taste of wine in all sorts of ways, and in different proportions.

The effects of ageing: from exuberantly fruity when young to very complex smells when very mature.

Be coherent, use your knowledge and common sense. Do not put a grape and an area together just because they seem to fit planted in that area. Do not associate expensive treatments with inexpensive wines (reduced yields with quaffing wines for example) or vice versa.

THREE COMMON MISTAKES

The first common mistake is to allow one specific element in your tasting notes to lead you towards the solution. Instead of ensuring that this particular feature is confirmed by the rest of your tasting, you desperately force the other elements to fit around it. I remember judging a friend of mine for a sommelier examination who, although a good taster, nevertheless fell into this common trap. Having convinced himself that he had recognised the aroma of a Barolo wine in what was merely a moderately expressive red wine, he went on to feel some firm tannin and a full body, when actually the wine was only slightly tannic and rather light. When struggling with a wine with little personality it is a mistake easily made, especially under the added stress of an examination. Remember, do not base your conclusion on just one single piece of evidence.

Another classic error occurs when your findings contradict your reasoning. Whereas in the preceding example you were unconsciously refusing to see some elements that would have destroyed your solution; here you register every aspect perfectly but your subsequent conclusion does not accord with them. For instance you note that a wine is concentrated and very ripe but you pick a mediocre vintage just because the wine seems to be of a particular age. Remember, your interpretation must tally with your observations.

The last fundamental mistake is when you narrow

down the options far too quickly and therefore do not give yourself enough possibilities from which to choose. I remember as a student assessing a very aromatic white wine, whose smell was of course a bonus as it gave me quite a lot of information to work on. The strong floral and apricoty-peachy aromas made me discard the possibility of a Sauvignon Blanc wine. This was confirmed by the moderate acidity, which in turn seemed to remove the possibility of a Riesling, coupled with the fact that the wine was quite full-bodied. I decided that I was facing a wine from Alsace. It could not be a Muscat as there were no signs of any grapey character, so I found myself hesitating between a Gewürztraminer and a Pinot Gris. I finally opted for the latter because it seemed to fit the bill better. I was wrong: the wine was in fact a Condrieu. Had a voice prompted, 'Have you thought of the Viognier grape?' from which Condrieu is made, I might not have got it right, but at least I would have stood a better chance. In fact, I should also have considered Albarino, Torrontes and other aromatic grapes. So from then on, before each session I would write a long list of grape names to extend my possibility. Remember, widen your scope and do not narrow down your options too early.

THE MYTHS OF BLIND TASTING

There are a couple of views on blind tasting that are regularly encountered in the wine trade.

You will constantly be told that your first impression is always the correct one. Like most tasters I have myself had that infuriating experience of changing my mind at the last minute only to regret it dearly. Nevertheless, I do not wholly agree with this theory. There have also been times when I changed my mind and was very pleased to have done so. Somehow when we modify our thoughts for the better, the first choice does not seem to linger in our memory with the same strength; it is almost as though the alteration were part of the thinking process. On the contrary, when we have changed from the right answer to the wrong one, the feeling of frustration is immensely powerful and it sticks in our memory for a very long time. It is a bit like a football manager who goes on and on about the penalty the referee omitted to give to his team but does not remember that perhaps a few games earlier his team benefited from the rather generous mood of a different referee. I would sum up by saying that if your first impression is a strong one, it is probably wise to stay with it, but if not feel free to change it if new ideas come to you. In effect, relying on first impressions reduces taste to instinct rather than reason!

The second view commonly encountered is that beginners are much better at blind tasting than accomplished wine-tasters. The theory is that their less cluttered memory makes them better suited to this type of exercise than the regular wine-taster who has a fully

stocked memory. All those years of training for nothing: what a depressing thought! Once again I do not entirely accept this point of view. Certainly it is not unheard of for a beginner to get the upper hand over an experienced wine-taster, but usually it happens at a social occasion and in a very short test. For instance in the course of a dinner the host may serve an unidentified wine and for fun ask the guests to name the wine. Of course if a wine professional is among the guests he or she will be expected to come up with the goods. Let's imagine that the wine is a Sancerre of reasonable character; the professional, having so many options of wine similar to a Sancerre might hesitate and opt for the wrong wine, whereas a beginner with little experience might give the correct answer because Sancerre is the only wine of that style with which they are familiar. Similarly on TV quiz shows an easy question can baffle an expert who may suspect a trap, while the novice doesn't hesitate because it is the only thing they know about the subject. But ask fifteen questions on the same subject or taste fifteen wines blind and it will soon be apparent who is the expert.

All sorts of legendary wine-tasting performances are regularly recounted. If this subject comes up in conversation, you can bet that somebody will know someone who is just incredible; you give him any glass of wine and in no time he will tell you what it is.

The raconteurs may indeed have once witnessed such a feat. The problem is that they put their faith in achievements like this occurring often, on the basis of a single successful session. If the first and only time I was watching a frame of snooker the winning player achieved a 147 I would probably think that it was quite a common occurrence. After all, that people should believe in the myth of blind tasters having almost super-natural powers is not surprising. Blind tasting is an activity that is hardly ever shown on TV, rarely written about, and yet frequently talked about. The mystery surrounding blind tasting makes it an ideal environment for legends to proliferate in.

THE LIMITATIONS

Blind tasting is not an exact science, and it's worth reflecting on what seem to be the main boundaries.

Young wines are easier to recognise than older ones. Indeed the aromas and flavours of the grape variety are at their maximum and have not yet been altered by the natural changes of bottle ageing. After a few years in the bottle, it is quite possible for an old red wine from the Rhône to smell like an old Bordeaux.

Aromatic grapes and those with a distinct flavour are evidently much easier to identify. You will have less difficulty in detecting a typical Riesling than a wine made from the Trebbiano grape.

Wine-making techniques which have a strong influence on the smell of the wine will render your job much more difficult, new oak being the obvious example, unless of course the technique used is specific to only a very limited number of wine areas. For example, although not completely exclusive to Fino sherry, the typical flor smell is quite useful in diminishing the options.

Certain wine areas seem to deliver specific aromas that are almost impossible to replicate. These are attributable to what the French call *le terroir*.

BLIND TASTING CAN BE FUN!

I hope all these complications have not deterred you from having a go at blind tasting, as it is extremely rewarding and can be great fun. Here are two spiced-up versions that are simple to undertake.

The most famous variation is the so-called 'option game', popularised by the legendary Lee Evans. A wine is served blind and three options are offered to a group of tasters; those who choose the right one stay in the game while the others are knocked out. The game continues until only one taster remains. For instance on serving a 1996 Chilean Cabernet Sauvignon from the Maipo Valley you could ask: is this wine A) European, B) American or C) Australasian?

The next questions could relate to the country (Argentina, Chile, USA), the region (Maipo, Maule,

Rapel), the grape (Cabernet Sauvignon, Merlot, Syrah), the vintage (1995, 1996, 1997) and if you are still left with more than just one player, the names of growers, alcohol levels or even colour of labels could provide additional questions. It is like the FA Cup of blind tasting, as the knockout system allows no mistake: players who correctly identified Cabernet Sauvignon but opted for Europe were defeated at the first hurdle!

The second version is played like *Call my Bluff.* Each member in a team of three gives their opinion on the identity of the wine just served, but two of them are lying and one has the right answer; you must decide who is telling the truth. The game usually covers several wines and works best when played in teams.

Finally, an analogy that perfectly encompasses the essence of blind tasting. In his book *The Official Guide to Wine Snobbery* Leonard S. Bernstein linked blind tasting with golf. He compared getting as far as the name and vintage of the wine estate to getting a hole in one; and encouraged tasters to be pleased with their performance if they managed to achieve par. In other words, if you have found the grape and the region (or simply the country) for some wines and for other more difficult ones you have found either just the grape or just the region (or country) and in both cases you have a fairly accurate idea of the vintage, you will have done very well.

Good luck in your blind tasting!

chapter 8

what makes a good taster?

Apart from a very small number of unfortunate people suffering from anosmia (inability to smell) or agustia (inability to taste), most of us are sufficiently well equipped to appreciate the subtleties of wine-tasting. Of course, as for any activity, some people will have better physical and mental aptitudes for it, but even for those seemingly less gifted, there is plenty of room to improve one's ability and reach a reasonable level.

TECHNIQUE

The first step to becoming a good taster is to learn the basic techniques so that you know what to look for in a glass of wine. By reading a book like this one or enrolling in a wine course, you should quickly obtain enough useful information to gain a basic but adequate technique, which you can then develop by practising. In the UK the Wine and Spirit Education Trust runs

some excellent wine courses for beginners that explain wine-tasting in a very professional but easy-to-understand manner.

WINE KNOWLEDGE

Relevant wine knowledge is helpful. You do not need to be a living encyclopaedia on wine; far from it, in fact, as too many wine facts can be of little use when you have a glass in your hand. However, learning the main taste characteristics of the more popular grape varieties, the main effect on grapes of local conditions, and also the few important wine-making techniques should set you on your way to achieving a tasting level that you can truly enjoy. Indeed it is much easier to understand how wine tastes if you can explain why it tastes as it does.

MEMORY

It is important to build up a wine-tasting memory of the main taste characteristics, especially but not only of smells. A good memory is crucial as it allows you to refer to the sensations you have slowly started to accumulate in your mind in order to compare them with and then recognise the sensation in front of you.

It is not just a matter of storing the maximum information, but rather knowing how to get the best out of it. Too much information, not properly assimilated, can prove more confusing than helpful.

If you are going to a wine fair where hundreds of wines are on offer, it is much better to taste less but analyse well, rather than trying to taste as many wines as you possibly can. When I go to a large trade tasting, for the first part of my time I try to find an interesting tasting theme and work on it. For instance, at the annual Californian wine-tasting, I might spend some time tasting and comparing the different Zinfandel wines exhibited. I am then able to form an image of the style and compare and contrast more easily than if I was tasting all sorts of wine styles in a short period of time. I spend the second part of the tasting in a less contrived mood; after all wine-tastings are not military camps!

CONCENTRATION

Directly related to memory is the ability to concentrate with enough focus and for long enough on one or several glasses of wine. Indeed your taste memory will only increase if you devote all your attention to the tasting session.

Not only do you need to focus exclusively on the wines, but also most of your attention should be directed at their relevant aspects. There is no point, for example, in spending much time on the appearance of a long line of young unoaked Sauvignon Blancs. Although you should give them a glance, appearance is not a crucial factor in that particular style of wine.

It is very important, too, that you can isolate your thoughts from your surroundings and both external and internal suggestions.

In chapter 1, which deals with the practical aspects of setting up a wine-tasting, I emphasised various elements of the surroundings. Obviously a noisy environment is not ideal but tasting rooms, especially large ones for standing-up tastings, are far from silent. You must therefore learn to detach yourself from what is going on around you.

External suggestions come from tasters around you, commenting on the wines. Opinions from other tasters are not very helpful if they are made before you have had a chance to make up your own mind as to the taste and quality of the wines. They will inevitably influence you in your individual interpretation of the wines. Once you have tasted the wines, though, comparing your opinions with those of experienced tasters can be very helpful, and may help in unveiling new angles that you had simply not seen or thought of.

Internal suggestions are those acquired through your own wine knowledge. For instance, prior knowledge that you are tasting a range of classed growth Bordeaux from a good vintage might influence you to find them automatically better than the range of wines from the very same estate but of a supposedly lesser vintage that you tasted earlier. The consequences are similar to those of external suggestions, except t hat it is much more difficult to protect ourselves from our own conjectures.

TRAINING

Regular practice is essential as it maintains good habits and reinforces the memory. If you go for a relatively long period of time, say six to twelve months, without coming anywhere near a glass of wine, or habitually devote little attention to the wines you are drinking, your tasting performance will be less sharp. Your concentration will be less, you might miss out some stages and thus some important aspects of the wines you are tasting. And on top of all this your memory will feel rusty. On many occasions you will find yourself thinking you know this smell but can't put a name to it, and you will feel frustrated. Even with constant training tasting is a difficult exercise, so not practising will only accentuate your weaker points. When you start tasting again, do not be fooled by a seemingly good performance. The natural euphoria of restarting any activity often at first brings with it superb results, which evaporate later, bringing you back down to earth when the excitement has disappeared.

CURIOSITY

To make progress you need to be curious. You must want to discover new sensations. While tasting the same style of wines over and over again might give you a good understanding, you will miss the points of reference and comparison to be found with other wines and may also become slightly blinkered.

OPEN-MINDEDNESS

Curiosity is a positive attitude in wine-tasting, so try to keep an open mind. You might not personally like a grape variety or a style of wine, but you should nevertheless still be capable of appreciating true quality, rather as a true sportsman acknowledges the quality of the opposition. Being biased and refusing to recognise other values will undermine your tasting expertise!

CONFIDENCE

Do not be afraid to stand by your opinion if it is based on a sound tasting assessment. You might be wrong, but you will learn more that way rather than just accepting a general view without understanding why. Of course nobody likes to make a fool of themselves, so you do not need to shout out your findings or seek to impose them. Confidence is not arrogance!

PASSION

Wine-tasting may become an all-absorbing passion; and why not? But even if it doesn't, a small amount of passion is necessary to enable you to confront the inevitable difficulties and encourage you to pursue your wine journey.

FUN

Wine is an important element of certain diets, in particular the Mediterranean one. It is also, as many of us have experienced, a reliable source of a hangover! However, if wine producers go to great lengths to improve the taste of their wines, it is because good wine provides a unique and extremely pleasurable sensation that can only be fully appreciated by tasting. But to maximise this pleasure, wine-tasting has to be approached with a sense of fun.

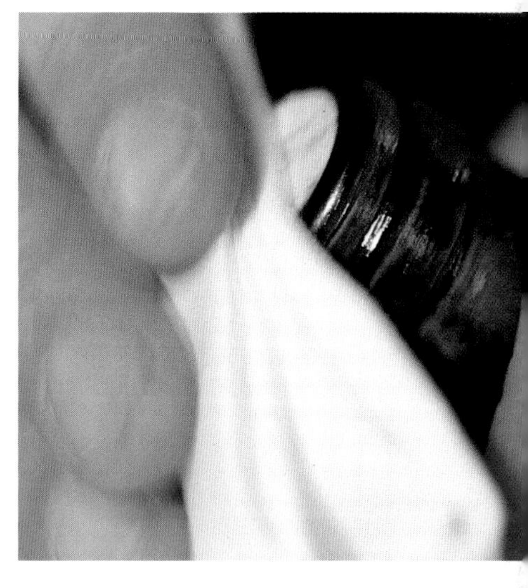

appendices

wine composition

WATER

Water is by far the greatest component of wine (and grapes) amounting roughly to between 70–90 per cent depending on the wine. It plays a vital role because it supports and balances the other wine components.

ALCOHOL

The second most important component is alcohol (mostly ethyl alcohol) from 8.5–15 per cent by volume. Alcohol originates from the transformation of the grape sugar (sometimes itself increased by the addition of external sugar) into alcohol under the action of yeasts. Some type of wines such as 'alcohol free' or 'low alcohol' have much less because it has been removed or reduced, and some fortified wines can have around 20 per cent because alcohol has been added to them. Alcohol tends to produce a slightly sweet and warm sensation in the mouth; in greater quantity it increases the feeling of weight and the viscosity of a wine but also decreases the perception of acidity and astringency. In reacting with other elements of the wine, it also plays a role in the wine's smell.

ACIDS

Acids represent no more than 1 per cent of a wine's content but they play a vital role in its taste. Acids are either fixed or volatile. Fixed acids are those that cannot be separated from the wine by distillation and volatile acids are those that can. Their sum in a wine is referred to as the 'total acidity'. The acid strength is normally measured by using the pH scale. Wines from very cool climatic growing conditions will have a low pH of around 2.9–3.1 and those from a very warm climate will have a pH of up to 4, with the majority of wines on a pH between 3.2–3.6. The lower the pH the crisper the taste, and wines with a high pH will often taste flabby. In addition the interaction of these acids in a wine will play a part in its aromatic make-up.

Of the fixed acids tartaric acid and malic are the two most important acids originating in the grape; citric acid is also found but in very small quantities. Wine-makers often convert the malic acid in wine into lactic acid (through the action of bacteria) by a wine-making technique called malolactic fermentation (MLF). Lactic acid has a softer feel than malic acid and so this operation is done for most red wines and for many smooth dry white wines. There are several other acids in wine – such as succinic acid (which originates from fermentation) – but they participate in a lesser way to the refreshing sensation produced by the overall acidity of wine. Wine high in acidity normally looks very bright and acids also contribute to a wine's smell. Acids produce a fresh feeling, which can make wine taste sharp or tart on the palate if the acid level is too high.

In well-made wines their action balances very sweet or high-alcohol wines and make them more palatable.

Acetic acid is a volatile acid originating from the action of yeast and bacteria, and is responsible for the occasional vinegary taste of wine (see the section on wine faults in chapter 4 pages 96–9). Every wine contains some acetic acid and it can even play a positive role in a wine's character but its level must be kept low (preferably less than 0.05 per cent).

SUGARS

The sugar content of wine (mainly fructose and glucose) can vary from 0.1–20 per cent. Sugars are found naturally in the grapes (a small external addition is permitted in some regions) and the riper the grapes the higher the level of sugar. The sugar left naturally in a wine, after fermentation or by its voluntary stoppage, is referred to as residual sugar. Not surprisingly, dry wines have only a very small amount of it, no more than 9g per litre of wine but often less (2–4g) depending on the area and style. Wines between 10–40g are referred as medium dry up to medium sweet. For sweet wines it can vary from 40g to more than 200g per litre of wine. Apart from very dry wines it is always difficult to estimate precisely the amount of sugar in a bottle of wine. Sweet wines look more viscous, especially when the glass is swirled, and often, though not always, have a honey smell. I will not surprise you by confirming that sugar does indeed produce a sweet and rich sensation on the palate. When the sugar content is above 5g per litre it can give them an added roundness and also masks any slight bitterness, which often sparks some controversy as purists argue that a dry wine should contain only the non-fermentable sugars (less than 2g per litre). As with most wine components its perception is greatly influenced by other elements. For instance the greater the level of acidity the less noticeable its sugar content. This is why the best sweet wines always have enough acidity to stop them becoming cloying.

PHENOLICS

Another important family of components are the phenolics. These are found in greater quantity in red wines (around 3–4g per litre) and include the colouring pigments, some flavour compounds and the tannins. They are extracted from the skins of the grapes during the maceration with the must. Pigments, called anthocyanins, give the colour to red wines once they have been dissolved during the maceration period, and they will carry on changing during ageing. The flavour compounds, along with other elements, contribute to the special odour of wine. Tannins give red wine its firm structure, its dryness and the puckering sensation felt in the palate referred to as astringency (not to be confused with bitterness). The extent to which they will be felt depends on how ripe the grapes were when harvested, the wine-making process and the state of maturity of the wine. Unripe grapes and stalks (if kept during fermentation), prolonged skin maceration during and after fermentation and strong pressing will produce tougher wines. By diminishing the level of tannins, fining operations will help to reduce slightly that tough impression. In addition during ageing the tannins change chemically (polymerisation and slow precipitation), making mature wines feel smoother. Finally, for those wines matured in new oak barrels, wood tannins are passed into them during maturation.

GLYCEROL

Glycerol, relatively important from a quantitative point of view (around 1 per cent in dry wines and up to 3 per cent in some sweet wines), is produced during fermentation. It has only a moderate effect on taste, however, seeming to increase only very slightly the smoothness of those wines with a higher content.

GASES

Several dissolved gases are also found in a finished wine. Carbon dioxide, a by-product of fermentation, is an indispensable constituent of sparkling wines. They contain large quantities of it and its role is fundamental to their visual aspect and taste in general. It is present even in still wines, although the amount is normally fairly low, around 200–500mg per litre, but it can be slightly higher in some young wines where more has been voluntarily retained or added in order to improve the taste of the wine. Apart from the visual aspect (possible in still wine if the level is on the high side, from 800mg per litre) carbon dioxide increases the sensation of freshness, produces tingles on the tongue, diminishes the perception of sweetness, increases a tannic sensation and augments the release of aromas.

Sulphur dioxide is of significant importance in wine. A minute quantity is produced naturally during vinification, but most of it is added by wine makers. It is used as an antiseptic and antioxidant. Its purpose is to protect the wine against deterioration through the action of bacteria or unwanted yeast, and against oxidation. The healthier the grapes and the greater the hygiene of the wine-making the lower the amount of sulphur dioxide needed. Its use is regulated and in the EU maximum levels are set depending on the style of wine. On average a still wine will have around 60–120mg per litre of total sulphur dioxide (called 'total' because there are two parts in wine, one combined and another free). Red wines usually have lower levels than white, because the greater amount of phenolics gives them more natural protection against oxidation. People suffering from asthma are particularly sensitive to sulphur dioxide and should consult their doctor for advice on wine consumption. High levels of sulphur dioxide tend to make white wines lighter in colour (as if bleached), the wine smells like a struck match, its aromas are neutralised, and both on the nose and in the mouth it produces a prickly sensation.

Oxygen is not normally present in bottled wine as it will have combined with other elements during wine making and maturation. However the contact of oxygen with must (grape juice) or wine and its control by the wine-maker during those periods will play on the wine's overall character. For instance very fresh and fruity dry white wines will have been protected and isolated from it as much as possible to avoid a darkening in colour and a loss of aromas. Full bodied red wines will benefit from time to time from a small amount of oxygen during maturation to soften them and prevent them from taking on a smell of hydrogen sulphide (see wine faults in chapter 4 pages 96–9).

VOLATILE ELEMENTS

The last category of wine constituents comprises the families of very volatile elements. These might originate from the grapes (terpernes), be formed during fermentation (higher alcohols also known as fusel oils, esters, ketones), be extracted from the wine container (aldehydes) such as oak or formed during maturation and ageing (esters, aldehydes). They perform a crucial role in the overall odour of a wine and are responsible, either individually or in combination with others, for the different fruity, floral and other smells found in wine. For instance the ester ethyl hexanoate is supposed to be responsible for the strawberry smell of some red wines, the terperne eugenol accounts for the clove smell found in some spicy red wines and the aldehyde vanillin gives some oak-aged wines their vanilla odour.

OTHERS

Around 1,000 other components have been found in minute quantities in wine such as methanol, calcium, potassium, iron, copper, phosphates, chlorides and some vitamins. No doubt they play their part, but they are less relevant to a taster because they cannot be isolated or perceived by tasting alone.

Finally, a few words on some important elements called fining agents. The most commonly used are bentonite (a type of clay), gelatine (made from animal parts), isinglass (fish bladder), egg white, or synthetic ones (PVPP). Wine-makers add one or more to clarify and stabilise the wine. Their function is to combine with unwanted particles of the unfinished wine and to precipitate these particles with them. Racking and filtering are then carried out to get rid of that mixture and to obtain clearer and brighter wines. Wine should not have any fining agents left once it is bottled, however, animal-based ones may be of concern for vegetarians or vegans, because it is possible that very minute traces of them are left in wine.

glossary of technical terms

Under this section I do not intend to give a long list of technical terms but only to explain very simply some important factors of production, those that seem to have the most effect on taste.

Additives: products added to the must or wine principally for conservation purposes such SO_2 or ascorbic acid
Alcoholic fermentation: transformation of grape juice (must) into wine through the action of yeasts
Autolysis (yeast): breakdown of yeast cells during maturation, giving the wine additional character
Barrel-fermented: technique used for premium-quality white wines destined to be matured in new oak barrels. Fermenting them in barrels gives them a more subtle integration of the oak flavours than if the wine was fermented in stainless steel and then put in barrels.
Barrel maturation: gives the wine a rounder structure and imparts some oaky flavours if new or partly new barrels are used
Biodynamic: organic growing in concordance with the movement of the stars following the principles of Rudolf Steiner
Bleeding: drawing off a small amount of the juice of a red must to increase the proportion of skins to juice
Blending: mixing two or more unfinished wines in order to get either a better one or a consistent style
Botrytis cinerea: fungus that attacks the skins of grapes, when detrimental referred to as 'grey rot', but can be beneficial for some sweet wines ('noble rot') giving the wine an extra dimension of flavours and texture, as well as concentrating the sugar
Bunch thinning: removal of some bunches of grapes a few weeks before harvest to concentrate the quality of the remaining ones
Cap management: red wine-making decision on how to treat the cap of skins during fermentation, pumping juice on top of it regularly, punching down the cap in the juice frequently or keeping the cap submerged into the juice are some of the options
Carbonic maceration: red wine-making technique used to produce some fruity and soft red wines by starting the fermentation without crushing the bunches of grapes and putting them in an atmosphere saturated in CO_2 in order that a proportion of them start an intracellular fermentation
Chaptalisation: addition of sugar to the must in order to increase the alcohol level of the final wine
Cold fermentation: used principally for white wines to conserve the maximum of aromas. It often results in wines smelling of sherbet and pear drops
Cold stabilisation: wine-making operation to avoid the precipitation of tartrate crystal later on in bottle
Concentration: wine-making technique employed to remove a quantity of water from the must or the wine in order to concentrate the proportion of the remaining elements
Cryo-extraction: a concentration technique which is based on the difference in freezing temperatures between the various elements of grape juice
Deleafing: removal of a percentage of leaves in order to increase sun penetration in the vineyard to minimise fungal diseases and improve the quality of the grapes
Destemming/destalking: red wine-making decision prior starting fermentation. Stalks possess some tannin that can give unwanted 'stalky' flavours and render the wine tougher
Eiswein: natural concentration of the grape juice through differences in freezing temperatures of the elements of the grape, by harvesting them late in the season at a moment when they are frozen and pressing them immediately
Entropy evaporation: concentration technique by evaporating grape must at low temperatures under vacuum to remove a percentage of water
Estufayen: specific heating process for Madeira wines during their maturation
Filtration: removal of suspended particles in the wine by putting it through filtration equipment. Filtration can be very coarse just to eliminate the visible particles up to very tight in order to intensely clarify the wine (sterile filtration removes yeast and bacteria)
Fining: addition of an agent into the wine in order to provoke a reaction and precipitation that will enable the stabilisation and clarification of the wine
Flash detente: technique using heat to increase extraction from red grapes
Flavour enhancing yeasts: selected yeasts used because they help to generate the production of aromas; however these do not normally last very long in the wines (six to twelve months)
Flor: wine-making technique used in Jerez for the production of fino sherry. The wines are matured under a veil of yeasts that protect them against the action of oxygen resulting in wine having some very specific flavours (e.g. green walnut)
Fortified: addition of alcohol in a fermenting must to stop its fermentation in order to retain some residual sugar and help protects the wine from refermenting.

Some dry wines can also be fortified to boost their alcohol level and give them a particular style
Free run juice: in white wine-making the juice that will drain first without pressing; it is of better quality
Free run wine: in red wine-making the wine that will drain first without pressing; it is of better quality
Hyperoxidation: white wine-making technique, oxidation of the juice prior to fermentation in order to eliminate some undesirable components
Irrigation: providing water to the vines; badly regarded by some wine experts because if done too generously can dilute the quality of the grapes
Late harvest: harvesting grapes when they are very ripe, even in a partial or very advanced botrytised state
Lees stirring (bâtonnage): operation done during maturation in order to remix the yeast cells within the wine to add extra character.
Malolactic fermentation: conversion of the harsh malic acid into the softer lactic acid through the action of lactic bacteria, makes the wine smoother
Micro-bullage: used for wines kept in stainless-steel vats, a small amount of oxygen is introduced into the wine in order to recreate the smoothness of oak maturation without imparting the oaky flavour
Oak chips: inexpensive process to impart an oaky flavour to the wine, however their use does not match the quality achieved with wine matured in new oak casks
Oak maturation: maturation of the wine in new or a proportion of new oak casks in order to impart appealing oaky flavours and to improve their texture (making it smoother)
Organic growing: grape growing without chemical fertiliser, fungicides and insecticides. The most extreme form is biodynamic (see entry)
Oxidative ageing: wine matured with a certain and regular level of oxygen contact, resulting in the browning of the colour and the creation of specific flavours
Passerillage: concentration technique in which grapes are dried out in order to increase the percentage of sugar
Pasteurisation: heating wine to destroy micro-organisms
Pre-maceration: operation prior to fermentation to help the extraction of flavours and colour for red wine
Press wine: wine collected after pressing the cap; it gives wine of lesser quality because too extracted, however a proportion of it can be advantageously blended with the free-run wine to boost the colour or the tannin level of the final blend
Protective wine-making: minimising oxygen exposure during wine-making to give fruitier wines
Pumping over: juice brought back and projected regularly on to the cap during the fermentation of red wines to increase extraction of colour and tannins
Punching down: cap pushed regularly into the juice to break it up and consequently increase the extraction of colour and tannins. Considered to be more gentle then pumping over
Racking: drawing off the wine from a vat or a cask into a new one in order to separate it from its lees. It can also be used to aerate the wine
Reductive ageing: wine matured and aged with minimum exposure to air
Residual sugar: the sugar left in the wine once the fermentation has finished or been stopped
Reverse osmosis: a concentration technique which uses the differences in molecular weight to separate a percentage of water from the wine by putting it through a membrane and exercising osmotic pressure
Second fermentation: sparkling wine-making technique to produce and keep under pressure some CO_2 into the wine.
Settling: clarification of white wine before fermentation starts
Skin contact: maceration of skin with juice prior to fermentation to extract more flavours for white wine
Spinning cone column: apparatus used for reducing alcohol in wine; a small percentage (around 10 per cent) is put through that device and is then later put back with the rest of the wine
Sur lie: wine matured on its lees in order to gain an extra dimension in terms of flavours and texture
Sussreserve: addition of unfermented grape juice in a wine to sweeten it
Terroir: French term including soil, climate and topography
Topping up: regular addition to a cask of wine to replace the amount that has evaporated
Whole bunch fermentation: red wine-making technique, the grapes are left unstemmed in order to get more complex flavours
Whole bunch pressing: for the production of many top white wines the grapes are pressed directly without any destemming or any crushing in order to get the best quality juice possible
Yield: the vines growing technique and the weather will greatly influence the yield. Therefore there is not an ideal yield, nevertheless a very high yield never produces top-quality wine

glossary of tasting terms

Acidic: wine that tastes sharp because it has too much acid
Aftertaste: the sensation after the wine has been swallowed or spat out (length and quality)
Animal: family of aromas (e.g. gamey, leather)
Aroma: referring principally to the smell of young wines. However in Burgundy the word aroma is normally qualified by the words primary, secondary and tertiary. Primary refers to the smell of young wine, secondary to the smell of wine-making and tertiary is equivalent to bouquet
Aromatic: wines with powerful aroma
Aroma wheel: diagram by Professor A Noble devised to help clarify tasting terms for aroma
Artificial: a not-very-elegant smell resembling that of a manufactured product; it can also describe the appearance of a wine that does not look very natural
Assertive: powerful nose but not very elegant
Astringent: high level of hard tannins provoking an unpleasant puckering effect in the palate as well as giving a fairly dry sensation
Austere: hard feeling in the mouth
Autolytic character: especially for quality sparkling wines, smelling yeasty because the wine has been matured on its lees
Backward: not as developed as the wine should be
Balance: the degree of harmony between all the wine's constituents
Bitter: an unpleasant taste sensation, usually leaving a bad aftertaste
Bland: weak and uninspiring smell
Blockbuster: very full-bodied wine with a lot of extract
Body: the weight of a wine (think of skimmed milk versus full-cream milk)
Botrytised: dessert wines having been produced from botrytis-affected grapes, giving them a luscious texture and some honey/roasted-fruit flavours
Bottle-age: special flavours gained from the chemical changes occurring during the reductive conditions provided by the bottle
Bottle-stink: stale smell sometimes noticeable in newly opened wine which usually disappears once aerated
Bouquet: the smell of wine that has aged and developed a beautiful character
Brilliance: the degree of brightness in a wine
Buttery: often an indication of a wine that has had malolactic fermentation
Chewy: wine lacking in smoothness, not dramatically unpleasant but definitely unbalanced in its structure
Clean: not smelling faulty
Clear: no cloudiness or haze in a wine's appearance
Close-knit: a light- to middle-bodied wine with some firm but ripe tannins
Cloudy: appearance marred by impurities or a haze
Coarse: poor structure, sharp or hard
Compact: very solid wine full of flavour with a lot of firm tannin
Complex: superb wine with a fabulous bouquet; unfortunately this term is sometimes used too loosely
Concentration: intensity of flavours in the mouth
Confected: a wine with a rather odd colour, not looking very natural, almost as if manufactured
Corked: very serious wine fault destroying the smell of the wine with unpleasant barky, musty, mouldy odours
Cloying: sweet wines with too much sweetness but not enough acidity to counterbalance
Crisp: very fresh and appealing sensation in the mouth due to a marked acidity, normally used for light dry white wines
Depth: rich in exciting flavours
Dried out: wine with no flavours left, just the acidity and/or the tannin
Dry: minimum level of residual sugar left in the wine
Exuberant: extremely aromatic wine
Fat: a wine with a very rich luscious texture
Firm: describes either the tannin alone or the whole structure of the wine; a positive description of powerful but ripe tannins or simply a full and solid wine
Flabby: insufficient level of acidity
Flat: poor structure due to not enough acidity. Also used to describe a sparkling wine that has lost its sparkle
Fleshy: fairly full-bodied wine, neither round nor totally solid
Flowery: family of aromas (e.g. rose, violet)
Fluid: very light to look at
Forward: a wine that has matured faster than it should have done
Fragrant: beautiful nose full of delicate odours
Fresh: nice acidity, similar to crisp
Fruit driven: full of youthful aroma
Fruity: should mean a family of aromas (e.g. apple, blackcurrant) unfortunately it has become a term meaning simply that the wine smells nicely appealing
Full-bodied: wine with a lot of weight and extract
Green: too much acidity making the wine sharp
Hard: too much tannin, making the wine tough
Harsh: negative structure; too acidic or tannic and also with a bitter finish

Hazy: wine suffering from a disorder (protein haze or a metal haze)
Heavy: very full-bodied with probably too much alcohol making it unbalanced
Herbaceous: family of aromas (e.g. grassy, hay)
Hollow: not dried out but lacking in flavours, especially compared to its nose which led one to expect more flavours
Immature: not ready to drink or not yet at its best
Intensity: related to either the degree of colour, the degree of smell on the nose or the degree of flavours in the mouth
Juicy: lively wine full of fruit with sufficient acidity but not too much, very fresh with plenty of flavour
Lean: lacking in flavour and body
Legs: traces left inside the glass after swirling, high alcohol wines tend to leave rich legs on the glass but it is an unreliable guide
Length: the impression after the wine has been swallowed or spat out (length and quality)
Light: related to the body, light wines normally (but not always) have slightly less alcohol
Long: related to the aftertaste, great wines have a long and beautiful finish
Loose: lacking in structure not unpleasant but could do with a bit more acidity or tannins
Luscious: very rich and smooth texture
Neutral: very little aroma but can still be enjoyable
Maderised: white wine that has oxidised, very dark in colour and flat in structure with unappealing flavours
Mature: wine ready to drink normally quite smooth in structure
Mineral: family of aromas (e.g. flint)
Mouthfeel wheel: diagram devised by the Australian Wine Research Institute to help clarify tasting terms for texture and feel
Oaky: smelling strongly of oak (e.g. vanilla, toast)
Obvious: inelegant smell (cheap oak), not faulty but lacking finesse
Opulent: full-bodied wine with a very smooth texture
Oxidised: wine that has been spoiled by oxygen, dark in colour, flat in structure and with stale flavours
Perfumed: very aromatic but in an elegant way, not as powerful as exuberant
Pure: superb smell of a great elegance and definition
Reduction: faulty wine smelling like sewage, garlic or rotten eggs
Restraint: a wine with potential but in a stage of evolution, going through a dumb moment
Rich: could mean sweet but in general is taken as a luscious texture
Ripe: very smooth texture or tannin
Robust: full-bodied wine with a solid structure
Round: full-bodied wine with a smooth texture
Scented: very delicate nose, very appealing
Sediment: visible deposit
Severe: hard, with too much tannin
Sharp: high acidity, unpleasant
Short: lacking in aftertaste once swallowed or spat out
Silky: very soft texture of great delicacy
Simple: not much character on the nose but not unpleasant
Smooth: rich and soft texture or tannin
Soft: delicate tannin or texture of a light- or middle-bodied wine
Solid: full-bodied wine with some firm but ripe tannins
Spicy: family of aromas (e.g. ginger, cloves)
Stalky: nose a bit vegetal and hard in structure
Steely: powerful structure for a full-bodied white wine with a marked acidity
Sulphury: faulty wine smelling of SO_2 and prickly both on the nose and in the mouth
Supple: light- to middle-weight wines with a delicate texture
Sweet: plenty of residual sugar
Synthetic: very inelegant smell, almost manufactured
Tannic: astringent sensation giving mouth-puckering and drying effect if too much
Tartrate: little crystals in wine resembling broken glass (in white wines) or small red diamonds (in red wines)
Tears: traces left inside the glass after swirling, high alcohol wines tend to leaves rich tears but it is a rather an unreliable guide
Tight: light- to middle-weight wines with dominant acidity (but balanced), or firm and ripe tannins
Tough: hard texture due to unripe tannins
Varietal: meaning that the wine is very representative of the grape's aromas profile
Vegetal: family of aromas (e.g. leafy), be careful as it can also be interpreted as slightly unripe aromas
Velvety: beautiful rich smooth texture of great delicacy
Vinous: does not smell of much just slightly alcoholic, not unpleasant but no recognisable character
Viscous: rich and heavy to look at
Volatile acidity (VA): wine fault causing wine to smell of nail varnish or glue
Woody: smelling strongly of wood, in particular of new oak
Yeasty: smelling of bread
Youthful: full of vitality on the nose and normally an immature colour.

bibliography

Books in which tasting is the principal subject:

AIS *Tecnica della Degustazione*, AIS 1995

Amerine, M.A. & Roessler, E.B. *Wines, Their Sensory Evaluation*, W.H. Freeman 2nd edition 1983

Beckett, F. *Wine by Style*, Mitchell Beazley 1998

Beckett, F. *Wine Uncorked*, Mitchell Beazley 1999

Broadbent, M. *Winetasting*, Mitchell Beazley revised edition 1998,

Brugirard, A., Fanet, J., Seguin, A. & Torres, P. *Tasting and Service of Vins Doux Naturels of Controlled Appellation*, Université des Vins du Roussillon 1991

Buffin, J. C. *Le Vin – Votre Talent de la Dégustation*, Hobby-Vins 1988

Bujan, J. & Artajona, J. *Tasting*, Freixenet 1995

Casamayor, P. *L'Ecole de la Dégustation*, Hachette 1998

Defranoux, C. *Apprendre à Déguster les Vins*, Solar 1988

Fortin, J. & Desplancke, C. *Guide d'Entrainement d'un Jury de Dégustation*, Edisem 1998

Fribourg, G. & Sarfati, C. *La Dégustation Connaître et Comprendre le Vin*, Edisud 1989

George, R. *Lateral Wine-Tasting*, Bloomsbury 1991

Gluck, M. *The Sensational Liquid*, Hodder & Stoughton 1999

Goolden, J. *The Taste of Wine*, BBC Books revised edition 1994

'Harper' *The Harpers Handbook to Wine Tasting & Entertaining*, Harper Trade Journals Ltd 1998

'Harper' *The Perfect Guide to Wine Faults*, Harper Wine and Spirit Weekly 1998

Leglise, M. *Une Initiation a la Dégustation des Grands Vins*, Editions Jeanne Laffitte 1984

Lenoir, J. *Le Nez du Vin,* Editions Lenoir 2nd edition

Meunier, Y. & Rosier, A. *La Dégustation des Vins*, Nathan 1998

Monnier, J. M. *L'Art de la Dégustation et la Decouverte des Vignobles en Pays de la Loire*, SILOE 1998

Murphy, D. *A Guide to Wine Tasting*, Sun Books Melbourne 1977

Paumard, B., Millet, J.G., & Gabs *Guide Pratique de la Dégustation* Eyrolles 2000

'Penfolds' *The Pocket Guide to Spotting Wine Faults*, Penfolds & Wine Magazine 1998

Pertuiset, G. *La Dégustation du Vin*, Quintette 1995

Peynaud, E. (and Blouin, J.) *Le Gout dû Vin*, Dunod 3rd edition 1996. English translation: *The Taste of Wine,* John Wiley & Sons, Inc 2nd edition 1996

Plumpton College *The Sensory Evaluation of Wine*, Plumpton College 1999

Pommier, A. *L'Art de la Dégustation des Vins*, Editions du Dauphin 1991

Poupon, P. *Plaisirs de la Dégustation*, Bibliothèque de la Confrérie des Chevaliers du Tastevin 1988

Puisais, J. & Chabanon, R.L. *Initiation into the Art of Wine Tasting*, Interpublish Inc 1974

Rabourdin, J.R. *Vocabulaire International de la Dégustation*, Elvire Editions 1989

Rankine, B. *Tasting and Enjoying Wine*, Winetitles 1990

Robinson, J. *Masterglass*, Pan Books Ltd 2nd edition 1987

Saint-Roche, C. *Le Goût et Les Mots du Vin*, Jean-Pierre Taillandier 1995

Schuster, M. *Understanding Wine*, Mitchell Beazley 1989

Sharp, A. *Winetaster's Secrets*, Warwick Publishing 1995

Simon, J. *Discovering Wine*, Mitchell Beazley 1994

Simon, P. *Wine-Tasters' Logic* Faber & Faber 2000

Spurrier, S. & Dovaz, M. *Academie du Vin Wine Course*, Mitchell Beazley 1990

Torres, P. *Le Plaisir du Vin*, Editions Jacques Lanore 1987

Vandyke Price, P. *The Taste of Wine*, Dorling Kindersley 1978

Vedel, A., Charle G., Charnay, P. & Tourmeau, J. *Essai sur la Degustation des Vins*, SEIV-Macon 1972

Vigne et Vin Publications Internationales *La Dégustation* & English translation *Wine-Tasting* both edited by Journal International des Sciences de la Vigne & du Vin 1999

Vivet. J *Goûter le Vin*, Christian de Bartillat Editeur 1993

Young, A *Making Sense of Wine Tasting*, Lennard Publishing 1987

Other wine books:

Adams, L. D. *The Commonsense Book of Wine*, The Wine Appreciation Guild Ltd 1991

Atkin, T *Chardonnay*, Viking 1992

Barr, A. *Pinot Noir*, Viking 1992

Barr, A. *Wine Snobbery*, Faber and Faber 1988

Bernstein, L. S. *The Official Guide to Wine Snobbery*, ELM Tree Books 1982

Bettane & Desseauve *Le Classement 2000*, La Revue du Vin de France

Brook, S. *Sauvignon Blanc & Sémillon*, Viking 1992

Brunet, P. L*e Vin et les Vins au Restaurant*, BPI Espace Clichy new edition 1996

Clarke, O. *Clarke's Encyclopedia of Wine*, Websters International Publishers 1999

Clarke, O. *New Classic Wines*, Websters/Mitchell Beazley 1991

Davidson, D. *A Guide to Growing Winegrapes in Australia*, Davidson 2nd edition 1995

Eyres, H. *Cabernet Sauvignon*, Viking 1991

Galet, P. *Précis d'Ampelographie Pratique*, Pierre Galet 1985

Galet, P. *Précis de Viticulture*, Pierre Galet 6th edition 1993

George, R. *The Wines of New Zealand*, Faber & Faber 1996

Gleave, D. *The Wines of Italy*, Salamander 1989

Halliday, J. & Johnson, H. *The Art and Science of Wine*, Mitchell Beazley 1992

Hanson, A. *Burgundy*, Faber & Faber 2nd edition 1995

Jeffs, J. *Sherry*, Faber & Faber 4th edition 1992

Johnson, H. *The Story of Wine*, Mitchell Beazley 1989

Johnson, H. *The World Atlas of Wine*, Mitchell Beazley 4th edition 1994

Johnson, H. *Wine Companion*, Mitchell Beazley 4th edition 1997

Joseph, R. *The Ultimate Encyclopedia of Wine*, Prion Carlton 1996

Lockspeiser, J. & Gear, J. *Organic Wine Guide*, Thorsons 1991

MacDonogh, G. Syrah, *Grenache and Mourvedre*, Viking 1992

Metcalfe, C. & McWhirter, K. *The Wines of Spain*, Salamander 1988

Mitchell, C. & Wright, I. *The Organic Wine Guide*, Mainstream 1987

Parker, R. *The Wine Buyer's Guide*, 5th edition, Dorling Kindersley 1999

Peppercorn, D. *Bordeaux*, Faber & Faber 2nd edition 1991

Peynaud, E. *Connaissance et Travail du Vin*, Dunod 2nd edition 1984

Pigott, S. *Riesling*, Viking 1991

Platter, J. *John Platter's South African Wine Guide 1995*, Mitchell Beazley 1994

Rankine, B. *Making Good Wine*, Sun Australia 1989

Remington, N. *The Great Domaines of Burgundy*, Kyle Cathie Limited 2nd edition 1996

Renvoise, G. *Le Monde du Vin Art ou Bluff*, Du Rouergue 1994

Reynier, A. *Manuel de Viticulture*, Lavoisier TEC & DOC 7th edition 1997

Robinson, J. *Jancis Robinson's Guide to Wine Grapes*, Oxford University Press 1996

Robinson, J. *Jancis Robinson's Wine Course*, BBC Books 1995

Robinson, J. *The Oxford Companion to Wine*, Oxford University Press 2nd edition 1999

Seely, J. *The Wines of South Africa*, Faber & Faber 1997

Stevenson, T. *The New Sotheby's Wine Encyclopedia*, Dorling Kindersley 2nd edition 1997

Sutcliffe, S. *Wines of Burgundy*, (Pocket Guide) Mitchell Beazley revised edition 1998

Waldin, M. *Organic Wine Guide*, Thorsons 1999

Wright, H. *The Great Organic Wine Guide*, Piatkus 2000

index

Entries in bold indicate glossary entries

author's acknowledgments

I would like to thank in particular six friends of mine who read the rough copy and gave me some valuable constructive criticism: Etienne Akar (also for his help as a voluntary and keen researcher), Tim Atkin, Henri Chapon MS (also for sorting out my computer predicament), Chris Foss, Lance Foyster MW and Bill Knott.

At one time or another in my career and on the very specific subject of tasting, certain people have given me some very useful information and tips and I would like to thank them: David Apel, Richard Bampfield MW, Jeremy Bennett, Paul Brunet, David Burns MW, Daniele Carre-Cartal, John Casson MW, Michele Chantome, John Downes MW, Serge Dubs, Philippe Faure-Brac, Dr Annick Faurion, Frederic Feyler, Vincent Gasnier MS, Neil Hadley MW, John Hoskins MW, Jane Hunt MW, Jean-Claude Jambon, Robert Joseph, Brian Julian MS, Claude Laage, Victor Ladonenko, Barry Larvin MS, Richard Lashbrook MW, Matthieu Longuere, Franck Massard, Patrick McGrath MW, Charles Metcalfe, Laurent Metge, Nick Mobbs, David Molyneux-Berry MW, Liz Morcom MW, Patrick Pages, Mark Pardoe MW, David Peppercorn MW, Fiona Roberts MW, Serena Sutcliffe MW, Geoff Taylor, Franck Thomas, Anne Tupker MW, Mark Walter, Clas Robert Wulff and Eric Zwiebel.

In addition I would like to thank my publisher Kyle Cathie and my editor Helen Woodhall both of whom have been fabulously supportive and extremely patient; Morag Lyall, copy editor, Geoff Hayes, designer, and Julia Scott, marketing manager, for their superb work; Jean and Tony Howe for providing a place where I could really have peace and quiet; Alison Thorne and Michael Sworder for allowing me to use some of the text I wrote for them in *How to be Your Own Sommelier* in 1997. Finally to my other business partner, Peter Chittick, my personal assistant, Victoria Norris and everyone else at Hotel du Vin, *un grand merci*!

publisher's acknowledgments

The publishers would like to thank the following for their kind permission to reproduce the following photographs:

5, 22, 26, 32, 35, 37, 40, 59, 62, 68, 73 and **74** Geoff Hayes; **79** James Sellers; **93** Geoff Hayes; **102** CEPHAS/Mick Rock; **106** CEPHAS/Wine Magazine; **111** James Sellers; **115** CEPHAS/Mick Rock; **116** James Sellers; **119** Geoff Hayes; **120** CEPHAS/Kevin Judd; **123** *bottom* Geoff Hayes; **135** Geoff Hayes; **139** James Sellers; **164** CEPHAS/Mick Rock; **171** Geoff Hayes; **174** James Sellers; **177** James Sellers.

Thank you also to all those at Harvey's Wine Museum, Bristol, for their kind permission to photograph not only the exhibits but also a tasting session in progress.